STUDIES IN ROMANCE LANGUAGES: 36
John E. Keller, Editor

Cervantes' Exemplary Fictions

A Study of the
Novelas ejemplares

THOMAS R. HART

THE UNIVERSITY PRESS OF KENTUCKY

Publication of this book was made possible
by a grant from
The Program for Cultural Cooperation
between Spain's Ministry of Culture
and United States Universities.

Library of Congress Cataloging-in-Publication Data

Hart, Thomas R.
  Cervantes' Exemplary fictions : a study of the Novelas ejemplares
/ Thomas R. Hart.
      p.   cm.—(Studies in Romance languages ; 36)
  Includes bibliographical references and index.
  ISBN 0-8131-1845-X
  1. Cervantes Saavedra, Miguel de, 1547–1616.   Novelas ejemplares.
  I. Title   II. Series: Studies in Romance languages (Lexington, Ky.);
  36.
PQ6324.Z5H37   1993
863'.3—dc20   93-4867

For ALAN DEYERMOND

Contents

Acknowledgments

John J. Allen of the University of Kentucky graciously read the entire manuscript. My colleague Steven Rendall made careful and constructive comments on earlier versions of every chapter. I also owe a debt of gratitude to the students in my graduate seminars on Cervantes at the University of Oregon, especially Jorge Casanova, Clayton Houchens, Caroline Jewers, Yolanda Molina, and Stefania Nedderman.

Parts of several chapters have appeared before in substantially different form: "Cervantes' Sententious Dogs," *MLN* 94 (1979): 377-86; "Versions of Pastoral in Three *Novelas ejemplares, Bulletin of Hispanic Studies* 58 (1981): 283-91; "La ejemplaridad de *El amante liberal*," *Nueva revista de filología hispánica* 36 (1988): 303-18; "Renaissance Dialogue into Novella: Cervantes' *Coloquio*," *MLN* 105 (1990):191-202. I am grateful for permission to use this material.

Introduction

Scholars usually divide Cervantes' *Novelas ejemplares* into two contrasting groups, just as they divide his writings as a whole into "realistic" works like *Don Quixote* and "idealistic" ones like *La Galatea* and *Los trabajos de Persiles y Sigismunda*. Preference for one or the other of the two groups has not remained constant throughout the nearly four hundred years since the stories were first published. The stories Rodríguez Marín edited for the *Clásicos castellanos* in 1914 include only one of those James Mabbe translated into English in 1640 (Riley 1981, 78-79). All of the novellas chosen by Rodríguez Marín come from the realistic group; none of Mabbe's do.

The opposition between the two groups of novellas is often seen as reflecting a chronological development from one kind of fiction to another, though *cervantistas* do not agree on the direction of the development. Amezúa saw Cervantes as moving from "idealistic" stories to realistic fiction (1956-58); more recently, Ruth El Saffar has argued that he moved in precisely the opposite direction (1974). Both make unwarranted assumptions about the order in which the twelve novellas were composed. Neither takes adequate account of the fact that Cervantes' career as a writer began in 1585 with *La Galatea* and ended in 1617 with the posthumous publication of *Persiles y Sigismunda*, two works that must surely be classed as idealistic or, in El Saffar's terminology, as romances rather than as novels. E. C. Riley probably comes closer to the truth when he suggests that "Cervantes never moved definitively from one kind of narrative to the other, but was liable to write one kind or the other or in some combination of the two to the end of his days" (1986, 13).

Amezúa, El Saffar, and Riley all assume that in the *Novelas ejemplares* Cervantes wrote two distinctly different kinds of fiction and imply that he did so consciously and deliberately. Indeed, Riley asserts that Cervantes "could not have written *Don Quixote* at all without a keen sense of the difference, and the relationship, between what we now think of as 'romance' and 'novel,' although he did not know any such terms" (1986, 11). The difference between the two kinds of narrative fiction may have been less clear to Cervantes and to his first readers than it is for modern readers; to divide the *Novelas ejemplares* into two opposing groups may be to read them in a way foreign to Cervantes' contemporaries. Perhaps we need to look for similarities among the *Novelas ejemplares* rather than differences. One such similarity is the attention given in all the novellas to the concept of *admiratio*, not "admiration" but "surprise" or "wonder." By making his principal characters temporary residents of marginal societies, like the underworld of Seville in *Rinconete y Cortadillo* or the gypsy camp in *La gitanilla*, Cervantes is able to present them as strangers in an alien world who are astonished at what they find there and thus to suggest to his readers that they should react in the same way.

We know very little about the way Cervantes' contemporaries read the *Novelas ejemplares*. One important piece of evidence is the *aprobación* by the Trinitarian friar Juan Bautista Capataz, which has been carefully analyzed by Bruce W. Wardropper (1982). Fray Juan was a personal friend and presumably stressed qualities in the stories that Cervantes himself wanted to see emphasized. His appraisal is, however, very brief. Any attempt to reconstruct the way seventeenth-century readers interpreted the *Novelas ejemplares* must be based largely on indirect evidence, usually fragmentary and almost always hard to interpret. In chapter 3 I discuss contemporary reactions to Heliodorus' *Ethiopian History*, particularly Jacques Amyot's prologue to his French translation (1547), that may help us to discover the qualities Cervantes' contemporaries valued in the *Novelas ejemplares* in somewhat the same way that the sixteenth-century commentaries on *Orlando furioso* throw light on contemporary reactions to *Don Quixote*.

I try, then, to read the *Novelas ejemplares* primarily in the context of the knowledge of everyday life and literary conventions shared by Cervantes' contemporaries. In my *Cervantes and Ariosto* I wrote that "we cannot read *Don Quixote* as its first readers did, and we would not want to if we could. There is no doubt that Cervantes' contemporaries failed to perceive, let alone appreciate, many qualities of his masterpiece that seem to us most evident and most valuable" (1989, 132). This is perhaps even more true of the *Novelas ejemplares*.

For George Hainsworth, sixty years ago, *Rinconete y Cortadillo* and *El coloquio de los perros* were valuable for their realistic depiction of everyday life (1933, 27). By contrast, *El amante liberal* seemed to him marked by "the almost complete absence . . . of the qualities of observation and realism that we noted in the first group. . . . In *El amante liberal* Cervantes reveals a certain familiarity with Moslem customs but the novella remains false and inconceivable for the modern reader" (ibid., 16-18). Jennifer Lowe concurs: "the plot is involved but with scant intrinsic interest and the various coincidences of capture, voyage and reunion are recounted with little zest". As a result, the novella "[fails] to make any real impact" (1970-71, 400).

Today we are in a better position to appreciate *all* of the *Novelas ejemplares*. We are in less danger of falling into what Northrop Frye calls "the sloppy habit of identifying fiction with . . . the novel" (1957, 303). Frye's studies of romance throw a great deal of light on Cervantes' novellas, as do the perceptive studies of pastoral by William Empson, C. L. Barber, and Renato Poggioli. Mikhail Bakhtin's discussion of the Greek romances helps us to measure the distance that separates *El amante liberal* from Heliodorus' *Ethiopian History*, while his conception of heteroglossia illuminates Cervantes' preoccupation with language in *Rinconete y Cortadillo*. The recent work of John Lyons and Timothy Hampton on example and exemplarity in Renaissance literature, like Susan Suleiman's on ideological fiction, touches on many points that lead to a fuller understanding of the *Novelas ejemplares*.

The novellas Rodríguez Marín chose for his edition are *La gitanilla*, *La ilustre fregona*, *Rinconete y Cortadillo*, *El licenciado Vidriera*, *El celoso extremeño*, *El casamiento engañoso* and *El coloquio de los perros*. C. A. Jones selected six of Rodríguez Marín's seven for his translation in the Penguin Classics in 1972, omitting *La ilustre fregona*. Harriet de Onís similarly picked six of Rodriguez Marín's seven for her translation, substituting *La ilustre fregona* for *El casamiento engañoso*. I have chosen the five novellas found in all three collections, omitting *El licenciado Vidriera*, which seems to me interesting primarily as evidence of Cervantes' continuing fascination with mental illness, and *La ilustre fregona*, which I think too similar to *La gitanilla* to justify a separate chapter. I have added *El amante liberal*, partly to give an example of the novellas Cervantes' contemporaries seem to have preferred but mostly because I believe that it is one of the most interesting of the twelve. James Mabbe's translation, *The Liberal Lover*, has been reprinted several times in the twentieth century. Mabbe shared Cervantes' delight in rhetorical display and made a valiant and generally successful attempt to convey its quality to his English readers.

Since this book is addressed not just to Hispanists but also to students of English and comparative literature, I include some material that will be familiar to Cervantes specialists and provide references to books and articles, in English wherever possible, that offer more extended treatment of points I touch on only in passing.

Quotations from primary sources are given both in the original language and in English. Quotations from secondary sources are given only in English. Translations are my own unless otherwise noted, though I have regularly consulted the translations of the *Novelas ejemplares* by C. A. Jones and Harriet de Onís and have occasionally adopted their rendering of a word or phrase.

References to the *Novelas ejemplares* are to volume and page number in Juan Avalle-Arce's edition. References to *Don Quijote* are to part, chapter, and page number in L. A. Murillo's edition. References to Castiglione's *Libro del cortegiano* are to book, chapter, and page number in Bruno Maier's edition; the translations are by Charles S. Singleton. References to Montaigne's essays are to book, chapter, and page number in V.-L. Saulnier's reissue of Villey's 1924 edition; the translations are by Donald Frame. The bibliography lists all the works cited plus a few others relevant to my work that I had no occasion to mention in the text.

CHAPTER 1

Teaching by Example

When part 1 of *Don Quixote* appeared in January 1605, Cervantes was fifty-seven and still virtually unknown as a writer. He had published nothing since his pastoral romance *La Galatea* twenty years before. *Don Quixote* was an immediate success. The Madrid edition was reprinted six times before the end of the year; within a few months there were pirated editions in Aragon and in Portugal (McKendrick 1980, 208). This popular triumph did not, however, establish Cervantes' reputation as a serious writer. Prose fiction did not yet enjoy the esteem given to poetry and drama. The creation of Don Quixote and Sancho hardly counted for much in such a scale of values.

Cervantes clearly felt he was an outsider in literary circles even after the success of *Don Quixote*. His lack of a university education may have contributed to his insecurity (Russell 1985, 8-9). *Don Quixote* had not made him rich. He could hardly have imagined that it would. Authors did not usually expect to make money from the sale of copies of their work; the real economic motivation for writing was the hope of attracting the attention of a wealthy patron (Cruickshank 1978, 800). Cervantes did not achieve this until some years later when he received aid from the Count of Lemos and a small daily stipend from the Archbishop of Toledo (McKendrick 1980, 289; Russell 1985, 21). Even then his rewards were modest, compared with those Lope de Vega received from the Duke of Sessa, whom he served as secretary, or those Quevedo received from the Duke of Osuna (Brown and Elliott 1980, 42).

When the *Novelas ejemplares* were published in 1613 Cervantes' situation was both like and unlike his situation in 1605. He must have hoped the novellas would enhance his reputation but his hopes seem to have been tempered by doubts about the reception of his new work. His concerns are reflected in the prologue, which begins by saying that he would have preferred not to have to write it:

> Quisiera yo, si fuera posible, lector amantísimo, excusarme de escribir este prólogo, porque no me fue tan bien con el que puse en mi *Don Quijote*, que quedase con gana de segundar con éste. [1:62]

> ⟨I should like, if it were possible, most benevolent reader, not to have to write this prologue, since the one I wrote for my *Don Quixote* didn't turn out well enough to leave me with any desire to write another.⟩

In the prologue to *Don Quixote*, part 1, Cervantes had presented himself as lacking the learning to compose a proper prologue. He therefore follows the advice of a friend who suggests that learning is not necessary: Cervantes needs only to take any quotation he happens to remember and attribute it to anyone he likes. If no quotation comes to mind, he can make one up himself. If he needs testimonials to the value of his work, he has only to invent them, and Cervantes proceeds to do this in the burlesque verses that follow the prologue, most of which are attributed to characters drawn from chivalric romances, including Amadís and Ariosto's Orlando. Some of Cervantes' contemporaries must have seen this part of the prologue as a sly dig at the ostentatious erudition of his rival Lope de Vega (McKendrick 1980, 199). His remark in the prologue to the *Novelas ejemplares* that the earlier prologue had turned out badly for him may refer to the hostility of Lope and his followers.

If Cervantes solves the problem of composing a prologue for *Don Quixote* by taking the advice of an anonymous and surely apocryphal friend, he puts the blame for having to undertake the distasteful task again on the failure of another nameless friend,

de los muchos que en el discurso de mi vida he gran-
jeado, antes con mi condición que con mi ingenio, el
cual amigo bien pudiera, como es uso y costumbre, gra-
barme y esculpirme en la primera hoja de este libro,
pues le diera mi retrato el famoso don Juan de Jáurigui,
y con esto quedara mi ambición satisfecha, y el deseo
de algunos que querrían saber qué rostro y talle tiene
quien se atreve a salir con tantas invenciones en la
plaza del mundo, a los ojos de las gentes, poniendo debajo del retrato: "Este que veis aquí, de rostro aguileño,
de cabello castaño, frente lisa y desembarazada, de ale-
gres ojos y de nariz corva, aunque bien proporcionada;
las barbas de plata, que no ha veinte años que fueron de
oro, los bigotes grandes, la boca pequeña, los dientes ni
menudos ni crecidos, porque no tiene sino seis, y ésos
mal acondicionados y peor puestos, porque no tienen
correspondencia los unos con los otros; el cuerpo entre
dos extremos, ni grande, ni pequeño, la color viva, antes blanca que morena; algo cargado de espaldas, y no
muy ligero de pies; éste digo que es el retrato del autor
de *La Galatea* y de *Don Quijote de la Mancha*. . . . Llá-
mase comúnmente Miguel de Cervantes Saavedra."
[1:62-63]

⟨one of the many I have won in the course of my life,
thanks to my circumstances rather than to my wit, a
friend who would certainly have been able to follow
the custom by engraving my image and depicting me
on the first page of this book, since the famous Don
Juan de Jáuregui has given him my portrait. Thus my
ambition would have been satisfied, and with it the desire of anyone who would like to see what sort of face
and figure belong to a man who dares to come before
the world with so many inventions, placing beneath
the portrait "The person you see here, hawk-nosed,
brown-haired, with a smooth and untroubled brow,
laughing eyes, and a crooked though well-proportioned
nose; a silver beard, which less than twenty years ago
was golden; a large moustache and small mouth; few

and poor teeth (for he has no more than six, and those
in bad condition and worse placed, since they aren't
opposite one another); an average sort of body, neither
large nor small; a good complexion, fair rather than
swarthy; with rather stooped shoulders and not very
light on his feet: this is the portrait of the author of *La
Galatea* and *Don Quixote.* . . . He is generally called
Miguel de Cervantes Saavedra.")

Cervantes follows this verbal self-portrait with a brief account of his own life:

"Fue soldado muchos años, y cinco y medio cautivo,
donde aprendió a tener paciencia en las adversidades.
Perdió en la batalla naval de Lepanto la mano izquierda
de un arquebuzazo, herida que, aunque parece fea, él la
tiene por hermosa, por haberla cobrado en la más
memorable y alta ocasión, que vieron los pasados siglos, ni esperan ver los venideros, militando bajo las
vencedoras banderas del hijo del rayo de la guerra,
Carlo Quinto, de felice memoria." [1:63]

("He was a soldier for many years and a prisoner for
five and a half, which taught him to have patience in
adversity. He lost his left hand to a harquebus shot at
the naval battle of Lepanto; he considers the wound
beautiful even though it appears ugly, since he received
it at the noblest and most memorable event past centuries have seen or those to come may hope to see,
fighting beneath the victorious banners of the son of
the thunderbolt of war, Charles the Fifth, of happy
memory.")

Cervantes' autobiographical sketch seems meant to persuade his reader that the book before him is the work of a
thoroughly respectable person. In terms of the three modes
of proof Aristotle distinguishes in his *Rhetoric* (1.2.1356a),
it functions both as ethos, by suggesting that the writer is
someone the reader can trust, and as pathos, by making an

emotional appeal to the reader's patriotism. This seriousness is, however, immediately undercut:

> Y cuando a la [memoria] de este amigo . . . no ocurrie-
> ran otras cosas que las dichas que decir de mí, yo me
> levantara a mí mismo dos docenas de testimonios, y se
> los dijera en secreto, con que extendiera mi nombre y
> acreditara mi ingenio. Porque pensar que dicen pun-
> tualmente la verdad los tales elogios, es disparate.
> [1:63]

> ⟨And if my friend . . . could remember nothing else to
> say about me, I would make up two dozen testimonials
> for myself and tell him about them in secret, thus
> making my name known and giving proof of my inven-
> tiveness. For it is absurd to believe that such tributes
> are truthful in every detail.⟩

The testimonials are not given; instead Cervantes' tone
once again becomes serious as he assures his "kind reader"
(*lector amable*) that

> los requiebros amorosos que en algunas hallarás son
> tan honestos y tan medidos con la razón y discurso
> cristiano, que no podrán mover a mal pensamiento al
> descuidado o cuidadoso que las leyere.
> Heles dado nombre de ejemplares, y si bien lo miras,
> no hay ninguna de que no se pueda sacar algún ejemplo
> provechoso; y si no fuera por no alargar este sujeto,
> quizá te mostrara el sabroso y honesto fruto que se po-
> dría sacar, así de todas juntas, como de cada una de por
> sí. [1:63-64]

> ⟨the amorous discourses you will discover in some [of
> these novellas I offer you] are so wholesome and con-
> form so strictly to reason and Christian doctrine that
> they cannot harm anyone, whether he reads them care-
> lessly or carefully.
> I have called them exemplary, and if you examine
> the matter attentively, you will see that there is not a

single one from which one cannot draw some useful example; and if it were not that I do not wish to belabor the matter I might show you the pleasure and benefit to be drawn from them all together and from each one considered separately.⟩

Cervantes underlines the seriousness of this statement by a return to his ethical appeal:

Una cosa me atreveré a decirte, que si por algún modo alcanzara que la lección destas novelas pudiera inducir a quien las leyera a algún mal deseo o pensamiento, antes me cortara la mano con que las escribí, que sacarlas en público. Mi edad no está ya para burlarse con la otra vida. [1:64]

⟨One thing I shall dare say to you: if I discovered that these novellas might awaken a harmful desire or thought in anyone who reads them I would cut off the hand with which I wrote them rather than expose them to public view. I am no longer at an age when one trifles with the life to come.⟩

The ethical appeal embodied in Cervantes' self-portrait in the prologue underscores the "excessive insistence" on the moral acceptability of the *Novelas ejemplares* to which P. E. Russell (1978, 447) and E. C. Riley have called attention. Riley notes that Cervantes submitted his manuscript both to the ecclesiastical and to the civil censor, though he was legally required to submit it only to the latter. He notes also that the text is preceded by no fewer than four *aprobaciones* and that there is reason to believe that the original title was *Novelas ejemplares de honestísimo entretenimiento* (1962, 101).

Scholars have been reluctant to accept Cervantes' claim that the *Novelas ejemplares* are morally edifying. Riley is not alone in feeling that "not all the *Novelas* are as innocent as [Cervantes'] declarations would lead one to expect" (ibid., 101). Juan Bautista Avalle-Arce shares Riley's doubts about the innocence of the novellas and concludes that Cervantes calls them exemplary because they can serve as artistic models for other Spanish writers (Cervantes 1982, 1.17). It is, however, unlikely that Cervantes' contemporaries understood his title to refer to the aesthetic excellence of his novellas rather than to their implicit moral teaching. No doubt some of his readers found it difficult to accept the notion that a morally irreproachable story may present immoral characters, as many people still do today. Others might have excused Cervantes on the ground that the morally questionable novellas offer *exempla vitandi*, examples to be avoided, as Montaigne slyly suggests near the beginning of his essay "Of the Art of Discussion":

> On ne corrige pas celuy qu'on pend, on corrige les autres par luy. Je faicts de mesmes. Mes erreurs sont tantost naturelles et incorrigibles; mais, ce que les honnestes hommes profitent au public en se faisant imiter, je le profiteray à l'avanture à me faire eviter. [3.8.921]

> ⟨We do not correct the man we hang; we correct others through him. I do the same. My errors are by now natural and incorrigible; but the good that worthy men do by making themselves imitable, I shall perhaps do by making myself evitable. [Frame 1958, 703]⟩

Why did Cervantes go to such lengths to stress that the *Novelas ejemplares* were not indecent? Riley observes that "the word *novela*, as well as being unflatteringly interchangeable with words like *patraña*, or 'deceitful fiction,' must have conjured up for the public the names of Boccaccio and Bandello and other *novellieri* well known in Spain, bywords for salaciousness" (1962, 102). Some of Cervantes' contemporaries may have considered the title *Novelas ejemplares* an oxymoron, like those of *La española inglesa* (*The Spanish Englishwoman*) and *La ilustre fregona* (*The Illustrious Scullery Maid*). Cervantes was by no means the only Spanish writer of the Golden Age who favored titles of this kind; the plays of his rival Lope de Vega include *Los muertos vivos* (*The Living Dead*) and *Lo fingido verdadero* (*What's False Is True*).

The shady Italian associations of the word *novela* may have prompted Cervantes to emphasize that his own novellas were morally irreproachable and that they were his own invention and not reworkings of foreign originals:

> Yo soy el primero que he novelado en lengua castellana, que las muchas novelas que en ella andan impresas, todas son traducidas de lenguas extranjeras, y éstas son mías propias, no imitadas ni hurtadas. [1:64-65]

> (I am the first who has written novels in the Spanish language, for the many others printed in it are all translated from foreign languages, and these are my own, neither imitated nor stolen.)

It was not just the Italian associations of the novella that made it suspect. Northrop Frye observes: "Any serious discussion of romance has to take into account its curiously proletarian status as a form generally disapproved of, in most ages, by the guardians of taste and learning, except when they use it for their own purposes. The close connection of the romantic and the popular runs all through literature. . . . Popular literature, the guardians of taste feel, is designed only to entertain: consequently reading it is a waste of time. More closely regarded by anxiety, it turns out to be something far worse than a waste of time" (1976, 23-24). In the Spanish Golden Age this distrust was extended to all works of fiction (Ife 1985).

There are other and perhaps more compelling reasons for Cervantes' refusal to make explicit the moral teachings to be drawn from his stories. Some of his contemporaries believed that the value of the moral teaching to be found in books was proportional to the effort of discovering it and reshaping it to meet one's own needs. According to Victoria Kahn, "The central assumption of the Humanist rhetorical tradition is that reading is a form of prudence or of deliberative rhetoric and that a text is valuable insofar as it engages the reader in an activity of discrimination and thereby educates the faculty of practical reason or prudential judgment which is essential to the active life" (1985, 11). No doubt Cervantes' contemporaries did not always read so earnestly. Montaigne himself writes in another essay that he seeks only pleasure in books, "Je ne cherche aux livres qu'à m'y donner du plaisir par un honneste amusement" (2.10.409). Sebastián de Covarrubias, in his Spanish dictionary of 1611, similarly considers reading a form of entertainment comparable to gambling or conversation, defining *entretenimiento* as "cualquier cosa que divierta y entretenga al hombre, como el juego o la conversación o la lectura."

Cervantes must have known the tastes of his prospective readers and been willing, at least up to a point, to cater to them. The prologue to the *Novelas ejemplares*, despite its stress on the moral benefit to be gained from reading them, explicitly asserts their value as entertainment:

> Mi intento ha sido poner en la plaza de nuestra república una mesa de trucos, donde cada uno pueda llegar a entretenerse, sin daño de barras; digo sin daño del alma ni del cuerpo, porque los ejercicios honestos y agradables, antes aprovechan que dañan.
>
> Sí, que no siempre se está en los templos; no siempre se ocupan los oratorios; no siempre se asiste a los negocios, por calificados que sean. Horas hay de recreación, donde el afligido espíritu descanse. [1:64]

> ⟨My intention has been to set up a billiard table in the public square of our nation where everyone can amuse himself without danger to anyone else.
>
> Indeed, one is not always in church; the oratories are not always full; people are not always engaged in business, however important it may be. There are times for recreation, when the weary spirit may rest.⟩

Bruce Wardropper (1982) connects this passage with the *aprobación* by the Trinitarian friar Juan Bautista Capataz

included in the first edition of the *Novelas ejemplares*. It is
likely that the *aprobación* presents a point of view suggested by Cervantes himself; Fray Juan was a friend, whose
poetry Cervantes praises in his *Viaje del Parnaso*.

Fray Juan declares that Cervantes' *Novelas* embody the
Christian virtue of eutrapelia:

> he visto y leído las doce *Novelas ejemplares* compues-
> tas por Miguel de Cervantes Saavedra; y supuesto que
> es sentencia llana del angélico doctor Santo Tomás,
> que la eutropelia [sic] es virtud, la que consiste en un
> entretenimiento honesto, juzgo que la verdadera eutro-
> pelia está en estas *Novelas*, porque entretienen con su
> novedad, enseñan con sus ejemplos a huir vicios y
> seguir virtudes, y el autor cumple con su intento, con
> que da honra a nuestra lengua castellana, y avisa a las
> repúblicas de los daños que de algunos vicios se siguen,
> con otras muchas comodidades, y así me parece se le
> puede y debe dar la licencia que pide. [1:55]

> ⟨I have seen and read the twelve *Exemplary Stories*
> composed by Miguel de Cervantes Saavedra, and since
> it is plainly said by the angelic doctor Saint Thomas
> [Aquinas] that eutrapelia is a virtue that consists of
> wholesome recreation, I judge that true eutrapelia is to
> be found in these *Stories*, for they entertain with their
> novelty [and] teach with their examples how to shun
> vices and practice virtues, and the author has achieved
> his intention, giving honor to our Castilian tongue and
> warning the nation of the damage that may be caused
> by certain vices, together with many other merits, so I
> believe he can and should be given the permission he
> requests.⟩

Now forgotten by everyone except a handful of theo-
logians, eutrapelia was well known to Cervantes' contemporaries (Jones 1985, 21-24). Eutrapelia is wholesome
recreation, *honesto entretenimiento* (Rahner 1972). It is
both a temporary turning away from more serious concerns

and a preparation for returning to them with renewed strength. The concept of eutrapelia thus dissolves the apparent opposition in the familiar Horatian doctrine that poetry should be both pleasant and morally beneficial: poetry is beneficial *because* it gives pleasure.

The narrator of the *Novelas ejemplares* rarely draws an explicit moral from the stories he tells. Cervantes generally entrusts the interpretation to one of the characters in the story, thus making the narrator's interpretation superfluous and at the same time demanding that the reader assess the character's ability to judge. Thus, at the end of *Rinconete y Cortadillo*, Rinconete himself pronounces judgment on Monipodio and his followers:

> Sobre todo, le admiraba la seguridad que tenían y la confianza de irse al cielo con no faltar a sus devociones, estando tan llenos de hurtos, y de homicidios, y de ofensas a Dios. . . . Y propuso en sí de aconsejar a su compañero no durasen mucho en aquella vida tan perdida y tan mala, tan inquieta, y tan libre y disoluta. [1:272]

> ⟨Most of all, he was amazed that they were sure they would go to heaven, despite their many thefts and murders and offenses against God, provided they did not fail to perform their devotions. . . . And he made up his mind to advise his companion that they should not remain for very long in a life so wretched and so evil, so hazardous, disorderly and dissolute.⟩

In most of the novellas, no explicit moral is drawn either by the narrator or by one of the characters.

Cervantes' contemporaries seem to have had relatively little interest in seeing how the details of a story fit together to constitute a unique meaning. They were apparently interested less in the story as a whole than in the individual incidents that constitute it. E. C. Riley notes that Cervantes' many remarks on fiction give "no hint of concern with the more recondite species of unity—the-

matic and symbolic as opposed to mere formal unity—
which it has been fashionable to find throughout his works"
(1962, 130). The sixteenth-century commentators on *Orlando furioso* divide Ariosto's poem into a great many episodes, each of which serves as a point of departure for
reflection on a moral or philosophical issue. They do not
as a rule discuss the relationship of one episode to another
or to the poem as a whole (Hart 1989, 115-16, 120). The
commentators have priorities of their own, as Daniel Javitch
has demonstrated (1991). Their endless arguments over
whether *Orlando furioso* is or is not an epic probably were
of little concern to most readers. But there is ample reason
to believe that most people did see Ariosto's poem—and
other works of literature—as an entertaining, and therefore
useful, source of moral instruction. The "sabroso y honesto
fruto" Cervantes promises his readers both in the individual
novellas and in the collection as a whole may be simply the
sum of the moral teachings to be derived from the innumer-
able incidents that form them.

Cervantes probably did not care greatly whether all his
readers interpreted the stories in the same way or as he himself might have interpreted them. Like other Renaissance
writers, he must have expected different readers to see them
as teaching very different lessons, asking only, as George
Sandys does in the preface "To the Reader" of his famous
translation *Ovid's Metamorphosis Englished, Mytholo-
gized, and Represented in Figures* (1632), that the interpretation be done "so as the principall parts of application
resemble the ground-worke" (cited in Allen 1970, 191).
Sandys' proviso implies of course that not just any interpretation will do. An author would feel perfectly justified in
rejecting an interpretation that made his work seem trea-
sonable or heretical. The writer's inability to control what
his readers make of his text was already a matter of concern
to Montaigne, who remarks in "De l'expérience" that "La
parole est moitié à celuy qui parle, moitié à celuy qui
l'escoute," "Speech belongs half to the speaker, half to the
listener" (3.13.1088; Frame 1958, 834).

Misgivings about how the *Novelas ejemplares* might be interpreted perhaps help to explain why Cervantes maintains so insistently that his stories are not morally harmful. John Lyons (1989) and Timothy Hampton (1990) have demonstrated the growing awareness on the part of many writers in this period that their works may be interpreted in more than one way. Lyons notes the decline of the traditional novella collection, in which the individual stories are embedded in a frame story that provides a perspective from which to evaluate the characters and their actions, asserting that the sixteenth century "witnessed the decline of the novella collection and the rise of the novel in its place. The novella is the genre that attempts or pretends to show the world through examples, while the novel in the seventeenth century centers on the vain quest for examples" (1989, 72). As a novella collection without a frame story, the *Novelas ejemplares* stand on the boundary between two different conceptions of fiction.

The importance of the change and the discomfort it caused some contemporary readers are clearly reflected in the controversy over the verisimilitude, or lack of it, of Madame de Lafayette's novel *La Princesse de Clèves* (1678). For these readers, as Gérard Genette observes, the notion of verisimilitude functions as "what we would call today an ideology, that is, a body of maxims and prejudices that constitutes both a vision of the world and a system of values" (1969, 73). To understand the action of a character is to see it as the embodiment of a maxim; conversely, an action without a corresponding maxim is incomprehensible (ibid., 75). Such actions do, of course, occur in life, but they have no place in literature because literature, as Aristotle teaches in the *Poetics*, is concerned with the probable, not the possible. Thus Bussy-Rabutin argues:

> L'aveu de Madame de Clèves à son mari est extravagant et ne peut se dire que dans une histoire véritable; mais quand on en fait une à plaisir, il est ridicule de donner à son héroïne un sentiment si extraordinaire.
> [Cited in Genette 1969, 71-72]

⟨Madame de Clèves' confession to her husband is extraordinary and is acceptable only in a true story; in a work of fiction it is ridiculous to attribute so unusual a statement to one's heroine.⟩

Bussy-Rabutin's judgment may be compared with the curate's appraisal of the interpolated novella *El curioso impertinente* in *Don Quixote:*

> Bien me parece—dijo el cura—esta novela; pero no me puedo persuadir que esto sea verdad; y si es fingido, fingió mal el autor, porque no se puede imaginar que haya marido tan necio, que quiera hacer tan costosa experiencia como Anselmo. Si este caso se pusiera entre un galán y una dama, pudiérase llevar; pero entre marido y mujer, algo tiene del imposible; y en lo que toca al modo de contarle, no me descontenta. [1.35.446]

> ⟨"This story seems to me good," said the curate, "but I cannot persuade myself that it is true; and if it is a fiction, then the author has made a mistake, for one cannot imagine a husband foolish enough to undertake an experiment as dangerous as Anselmo's. If it were a question of a lover and his lady it might be conceivable; but between a husband and his wife it seems incredible; as for the way it is told, it does not displease me."⟩

Like Bussy-Rabutin the curate believes that a work of fiction should be credible, that is, it should represent what usually happens. Both *El curioso impertinente* and *La Princesse de Clèves* challenge this notion of verisimilitude; perhaps for this reason Cervantes does not incorporate the novella into the main narrative of *Don Quixote*, like the story of Marcela and Grisóstomo or that of Dorotea, but presents it precisely as a work of fiction and one, moreover, that he pretends was composed by someone else.

Genette distinguishes three types of narrative. In the first, which he calls verisimilar, motivation is only implicit;

La Princesse de Clèves is an example. In the second, which he calls motivated, a character's reasons for acting in a particular way are justified by reference to his or her habits. Sometimes they are presented as typical not of an individual but of a class, as often in the novels of Balzac. In the third type, which Genette calls arbitrary, no motive is given even for the most extraordinary actions, as Stendhal makes no attempt to account for Julien Sorel's attempt to murder Madame de Rênal in *Le Rouge et le noir.* As Genette observes, there is no formal difference between the first and third types, so that the three types may be reduced to two. All narratives are either motivated or unmotivated; the latter may be subdivided into those that are verisimilar and those that are arbitrary.

When motivation is made explicit in the *Novelas ejemplares,* it is often proved false. *La gitanilla* begins with the assertion that gypsies seem born to be thieves, "parece que los gitanos y gitanas solamente nacieron en el mundo para ser ladrones" (1:73). The assertion is softened, however, by the introductory phrase *parece que,* it seems that, and is apparently contradicted by the following description of Preciosa's virtues, though the contradiction is only apparent, since we eventually learn that Preciosa was not born a gypsy.

Most of Cervantes' novellas are of the second, unmotivated kind. According to Monique Joly (1983), *La ilustre fregona* plays upon the unsavory reputation of girls who work in inns, epitomized in proverbs like these, cited in Gonzalo Correas's great collection of 1627: "figa verdal i moza de ostal, palpándose madura," green figs and inn maids ripen with handling, and "no konpres asno de rrekuero, ni te kases kon hixa de mesonero," don't buy a donkey from a muleteer nor marry an innkeeper's daughter (1967, 340, 257). (Correas advocated orthographic reform; I cite the proverbs in his idiosyncratic spelling.) Cervantes cites neither of these proverbs; if the reader is reminded of them it is because of the contrast between the virtuous Costanza, the illustrious scullery maid of the title, and the two "real" *mozas de mesón,* la Argüello and la Gallega. As in *La gitanilla,* the

maxims, what everybody knows, turn out to be both true
and false.

It is hard to distinguish the novellas that are verisimilar
from those that are arbitrary; often both types are combined
in a single novella. *El celoso extremeño* may be seen as an
amplification of the proverb "marido zeloso, nunka tiene
rreposo," a jealous husband knows no rest (Correas 1967,
526). Leonora's refusal to try to persuade her husband of her
innocence in the same novella similarly rests on a maxim
cited by Sancho in *Don Quixote* (2.43.364): "a 'idos de mi
kasa,' i 'ké keréis kon mi muxer?,' no ai responder," there is
no reply to "get out of my house" and "what are you doing
with my wife?" (Correas 1967, 4). By contrast Carrizales' decision to forgive his wife corresponds to no maxim; he himself explicitly presents it as extraordinary, saying that "la
venganza que pienso tomar de esta afrenta no es ni ha de ser
de las que ordinariamente suelen tomarse" (2:218), as Madame de Lafayette's heroine assures her husband: "Je vais
vous faire un aveu que l'on n'a jamais fait à un mari" (cited
by Genette 1969, 75).

Actions that correspond to no maxim produce admiratio,
a concept to which Cervantes and his contemporaries at-
tached great importance. E. C. Riley defines it as "a sort
of excitement stimulated by whatever was exceptional,
whether because of its novelty, its excellence, or other extreme characteristics" (1962, 89; see also Riley 1963.) The
writers and readers of Renaissance fiction, like the metaphy-
sicians of Jorge Luis Borges' imaginary Tlön, do not seek
truth or even plausibility but astonishment, "no buscan la
verdad ni siquiera la verosimilitud: buscan el asombro"
(1961, 23).

Cervantes uses both the noun *admiración* and the verb
admirar repeatedly in the *Novelas ejemplares*, as he does
also in *Don Quixote*. His characters often see or hear something that causes them to feel admiración, a sure sign that
the reader is supposed to feel it too. In *La fuerza de la sangre*, we are told that "*Admirados* quedaron de tanta cris-
tiandad los abuelos, pero la madre quedó más *admirada*"

(2:160; my italics), "the grandparents were astonished at such a display of Christian charity, but the mother's astonishment was even greater." In *Rinconete and Cortadillo*, the youthful protagonists astonish the innkeeper's wife with their good manners, "dejando . . . a la ventera *admirada* de la buena crianza de los pícaros" (1:225). In *La ilustre fregona*, the innkeeper tells the Corregidor he is about to hear things that will both delight and astonish him, "oirá vuesa merced cosas que, juntamente con darle gusto, le *admiren*" (3:103). Later in the same novella, the words spoken by the young gentleman turned stableboy provoke astonishment (*admiración*) in all who hear them (3:117).

Montaigne was fascinated by unusual events because of the conviction expressed in his essay "Of Experience" that "Il y a peu de relation de nos actions, qui sont en perpetuelle mutation, avec les loix fixes et immobiles," "There is little relation between our actions, which are in perpetual mutation, and fixed and immutable laws" (3.13.1066; Frame 1958, 816). The *Novelas ejemplares* remain poised on the borderline between a conception of verisimilitude that insisted that fiction must rest upon a body of familiar maxims and a fascination with actions that admit no explanation because they go counter to accepted norms. Cervantes offers his readers a world of wonders and in doing so prepares the way for the arbitrariness that marks much twentieth-century fiction.

CHAPTER 2

Exemplary Adventures: *La gitanilla* and *La ilustre fregona*

La gitanilla is the longest of the *Novelas ejemplares*. It is also the only one that contains a considerable amount of original verse, like the pastoral romances of the preceding century, including Cervantes' own *Galatea*. He may have placed it at the beginning of the collection to reassure his readers by offering a kind of fiction with which they were familiar.

The protagonist is a young nobleman, Don Juan de Cárcamo, with whom many of Cervantes' readers would have found it easy to identify. Many of those who bought recreational books (*libros de entretenimiento*) were members of the petty nobility, the *hidalgos*. They constituted the primary audience for the romances of chivalry, in which they found a picture of the kind of society in which they would have preferred to live, "a world that has no place for the merchant, where money is of no importance, where the city, the site of the economic activities of the bourgeoisie, never appears" (Chevalier 1976, 98). The city, where money is all important, almost always appears in the *Novelas ejemplares* in an unfavorable light, as Seville does in *Rinconete y Cortadillo* and *El coloquio de los perros*. One of the few glimpses of it in *La gitanilla* comes near the beginning, when a group of gypsies is invited into a nobleman's house in Madrid to sing and dance. Their hosts have no money with which to reward them, prompting Preciosa, the pretty gypsy girl of the title, to observe that in the world of the court everything must be paid for, even public offices:

Coheche vuesa merced, señor teniente; coheche, y
tendrá dineros, y no haga usos nuevos, que morirá de
hambre. Mire, señora: por ahí he oído decir . . . que de
los oficios se ha de sacar dineros para pagar las conde-
naciones de las residencias y para pretender otros car-
gos. [1:95]

⟨Take bribes, lieutenant; take bribes, and you'll have
money. Don't try to start a new fashion, for you'll die
of hunger. Listen well, my lady: I've heard . . . that you
must make money from an office so that when your
term is over you will be able to pay the fine for wrongdoing and get another post.⟩

Don Juan de Cárcamo is in Madrid because his father is
there trying to arrange appointment to a government job
(1:97-98), presumably by the same means Preciosa recommends to her hosts.

Most of the story takes place outside Madrid and in a very
different world. Preciosa insists that Don Juan must live
among the gypsies for two years before she will consent to
become his wife. To conceal his identity he adopts the name
Andrés Caballero; his new surname, like his behavior
throughout the story, indicates his continuing allegiance to
the ideals of his class. I shall follow Cervantes' practice and
call him Andrés until he resumes his true identity at the
end of the story.

Among the gypsies Andrés uses his money to keep his
honor as a nobleman intact. He insists that he needs train-
ing if he is to become an accomplished thief and that he
must not be forced to steal anything before a month has
passed (1:122). In reality, like the nobleman he is, "corres-
pondiendo a su buena sangre" (1:125), Andrés never steals
anything at all. He simply buys the things he claims to have
stolen and turns them over to the gypsies. He is so moved by
the victims of the gypsies' thefts that he sometimes repays
them out of his own pocket despite the protests of his new
companions, who insist that charity has no place in their
code of behavior.

Andrés' success in his role as gypsy is not solely the result of his wealth but of the personal qualities—courage, good looks, and physical dexterity—expected of a nobleman. His courtship of Preciosa is for him an adventure that enables him to demonstrate his innate superiority in all sorts of new situations. By linking the first of the *Novelas ejemplares* with the romances of chivalry, Cervantes displays a sure sense of his readers' tastes. Maxime Chevalier notes that "the romances of chivalry reveal a conception of love that is certainly refined but very different from that exalted by Plato and his followers. [It differs] above all in its adventurous and heroic aspect. Love in *Amadís* is not passion but action. It is a sentiment that leads a man to accomplish great feats that will enable him to win the love of his lady" (1974, 42).

For Andrés his new identity as a gypsy is a form of play. Like all play it must be taken seriously and is subject to precisely defined rules. The kinds of elegant play that occupy so much of a courtier's time are given a good deal of attention in Castiglione's *Book of the Courtier*. The participants in Castiglione's nostalgic dialogue are especially interested in the wearing of disguises. Signor Pallavicino observes:

Nel paese nostro di Lombardia . . . molti gentilomini giovani trovansi, che le feste ballano tutto 'l dì nel sole coi villani e con essi giocano a lanciar la barra, lottare, correre e saltare; ed io non credo che sia male, perché ivi non si fa paragone della nobilità, ma della forza e destrezza, nelle qual cose spesso gli omini di villa non vaglion meno che i nobili; e par che quella domestichezza abbia in sé una certa liberalità amabile. [2.10.204]

⟨In our Lombard country . . . there are many young gentlemen who, on festive occasions, dance all day in the sun with peasants, and play with them at throwing the bar, wrestling, running, and jumping. And I do not think this amiss, because then the contest is not one of nobility, but one of strength and agility, at which villagers are quite as good as nobles, and such familiarity would seem to have about it a certain charming liberality. [Singleton 1959, 101]⟩

Messer Federico objects that anyone determined to compete against peasants must be almost perfectly sure of winning, since he gains very little if he wins and loses a great deal if he does not. Even in dancing the courtier must always maintain a certain dignity; he should not attempt "those quick movements of foot and those double steps which we find most becoming in our Barletta, but which would perhaps little befit a gentleman" (2.11.205-206; Singleton 1959, 102). The courtier may experiment with such steps in private or in the company of a small group of friends but he should not attempt them in public unless he is taking part in a masquerade. In that case, according to Federico, there is no harm even if everyone recognizes him,

> perché lo esser travestito porta seco una certa libertà e licenzia, la quale tra le altre cose fa che l'omo po pigliare forma di quello in che si sente valere, ed usar diligenza ed attillatura circa la principal intenzione della cosa in che mostrar si vole, ed una certa sprezzatura circa quello che non importa. [2.11.206]

> ⟨because masquerading carries with it a certain freedom and license, which among other things enables one to choose the role in which he feels most able, and to bring diligence and a care for elegance into that principal aim, and to show a certain nonchalance in what does not matter. [Singleton 1959, 103]⟩

Andrés demonstrates his ability to excel in precisely the ways mentioned by Pallavicino:

> A doquiera que llegaban [los gitanos], él se llevaba el precio y las apuestas de corredor y de saltar más que ninguno; jugaba a los bolos y a la pelota extremada-

mente; tiraba la barra con mucha fuerza y singular
destreza; finalmente, en poco tiempo voló su fama por
toda Extremadura, y no había lugar donde no se hablase
de la gallarda disposición del gitano Andrés Caballero y
de sus gracias y habilidades. [1:126]

(Wherever the gypsies went, he won the prize and the
money bet on him as a runner and jumper; he played
bowls and *pelota* extremely well; he threw the bar with
great strength and exceptional accuracy; before long
his fame had spread throughout Extremadura and there
was no village where people did not talk about the
dashing gypsy Andrés Caballero and his graces and
accomplishments.)

In adopting for a time the role of the gypsy Andrés Caballero, Don Juan de Cárcamo can enjoy the "freedom and li-
cense" Castiglione's courtiers associate with masquerade.
But this freedom is, of course, not absolute. Andrés always
remains aware that his honor as a nobleman sets strict lim-
its on what he can do in his disguise as a gypsy.

Like Andrés, though with less apparent justification, at
least until her identity is revealed at the end of the story,
Preciosa is always conscious that she is playing a role she
has chosen for herself. Though the life of the gypsy tribe is
the only one she has ever known, she keeps aloof from it in
a way that suggests she regards it only as an interlude. She
refuses to acknowledge the authority of the gypsy chief, who
is quite willing to give her to Andrés in marriage, since it is
obvious that Andrés is wealthy. Preciosa insists not only
that Andrés prove his devotion to her by spending two years
with the gypsies before she marries him but also that their
marriage must not be subject to the gypsy law that a husband whose wife no longer pleases him is free to leave her
and marry a younger woman.

Cervantes describes Preciosa on her first appearance as

la más única bailadora que se hallaba en todo el gita-
nismo, y la más hermosa y discreta que pudiera hal-

larse, no entre los gitanos, sino entre cuantas hermosas
y discretas pudiera pregonar la fama. Ni los soles, ni los
aires, ni las inclemencias del cielo a quien más que
otras gentes están sujetos los gitanos, pudieron deslus-
trar su rostro ni curtir las manos;y lo que es más, que
la crianza tosca en que se criaba no descubría en ella
sino ser nacida de mayores prendas que de gitana,
porque era en extremo cortés y bien razonada. Y, con
todo esto, era algo desenvuelta; pero no de modo que
descubriese algún género de deshonestidad; antes, con
ser aguda, era tan honesta, que en su presencia no
osaba alguna gitana, vieja ni moza, cantar cantares las-
civos ni decir palabras no buenas. [1:74]

⟨the best dancer of all the gypsies and the most beautiful and discreet young woman to be found anywhere
and not just among the gypsies. Neither sun nor wind
nor other extremes of weather, to which gypsies are
more exposed than anyone else, could darken her face
nor roughen her hands. Moreover, the harsh conditions
in which she had been brought up showed that she
came of better than gypsy stock, for she was extremely
courteous and well spoken. In addition to all this, she
was quite self-confident, although not at all brazen but
on the contrary so virtuous, for all her boldness, that
no gypsy woman, old or young, dared sing bawdy songs
or use coarse language when she was present.⟩

It is no wonder Preciosa captures the hearts of all who see
her (1:75) or that some of them think it a pity she is a gypsy,
since she clearly deserves to be the daughter of a great nobleman: "¡Lástima es que esta mozuela sea gitana! En verdad, en verdad que merecía ser hija de un gran señor" (1:77).
No reader familiar with the conventions of romance will be
surprised to learn at the end of the story that Preciosa is indeed a nobleman's daughter, kidnapped in infancy by the old
gypsy woman she calls her grandmother.

Cervantes constantly stresses the distance that separates
Preciosa from her surroundings. His treatment of her is just

the opposite of the "atmospheric realism" Erich Auerbach analyzes in the novels of Balzac. Auerbach observes that Balzac's description in *Le Père Goriot* of Madame Vauquer's boarding house and its proprietor "not only . . . places the human beings whose destiny he is seriously relating, in their precisely defined historical and social setting, but also conceives this connection as a necessary one: to him every milieu becomes a moral and physical atmosphere which impregnates the landscape, the dwelling, furniture, implements, clothing, physique, character, surroundings, ideas, activities, and fates of men" (1953, 473). The contrast between Preciosa and the other members of the gypsy tribe is often seen simply as an instance of highlighting an idealized character by placing him or her against a realistically observed background. Cervantes' treatment of the gypsies is, however, no more realistic than his treatment of Preciosa herself.

Most of the gypsy chief's long speech of welcome to Andrés, in which he explains gypsy customs to his guest, is a mosaic of commonplaces drawn from the long tradition of literary pastoral:

> Nosotros guardamos inviolablemente la ley de la amistad. . . . Los montes nos ofrecen leña de balde; los árboles, frutas; . . . las fuentes, agua. . . . No nos fatiga el temor de perder la honra, ni nos desvela la ambición de acrecentarla. . . . Tenemos lo que queremos, pues nos contentamos con lo que tenemos. [1:118-20]

> ⟨We keep the law of friendship. The forests offer us firewood for the taking; the trees, fruit; the springs, water. . . . We have everything we want, since we are satisfied with what we have.⟩

The last sentence reveals the ironic displacement Cervantes introduces into his treatment of a central theme of the pastoral tradition. The gypsies find it easy to content themselves with what they have, since they have no scruples about stealing whatever they want. Taken in isolation, the gypsy chief's claim that his people do not live in fear of losing their honor may seem to echo Torquato Tasso's assertion in his pastoral drama *Aminta* that honor is the sole cause of all man's unhappiness, and indeed there is a sense in which for the gypsies, as for the shepherds of Tasso's Golden Age, whatever pleases is lawful (*s'ei piace, ei lice*). It is not, however, the same sense. In the context of his whole speech, the gypsy's remark amounts simply to saying that a man need not worry about losing something he has never bothered to acquire.

The gypsy chief's reference to honor is not the only disturbing detail in his speech. His long list of nature's gifts includes the fact that the fields offer his people vegetables, the vineyards grapes, and the reserves game, but though the gypsies proudly call themselves lords of the woods and fields, the woods belong to other men and the crops are produced by other men's labor. The gypsy chief departs still further from the tradition of literary pastoral by asserting that his people are not afflicted by the bitter scourge of jealousy (*la amarga pestilencia de los celos*). Most shocking of all is his assertion that among the gypsies there are many cases of incest though none of adultery, "entre nosotros, aunque hay muchos incestos, no hay ningún adulterio" (1:118). The fidelity of gypsy wives is well attested, but the accusation that gypsies routinely practice incest is pure invention. It is not, however, Cervantes' invention. Such charges were common in his day and were still being repeated a century and a half later (Leblon 1985, 43, 53).

Seventeenth-century Spaniards feared and despised gypsies, as many Spaniards do today (Pitt-Rivers 1961, 186). Their hatred is evident in the long series of laws that attempted to force the gypsies to give up their nomadic life and their distinctive dress and speech (Amezúa 1956-58, 2:6-9; Domínguez Ortiz 1971, 165-66). The first sentence of *La gitanilla*, in which the word *ladrón* (thief) occurs five times, must have seemed to Cervantes' contemporaries merely a statement of an obvious truth.

Although most Spaniards believed all gypsies were thieves, very few would have known anything about the life of a gypsy tribe. Cervantes may have set his novella among the gypsies partly for this reason.He was probably familiar with Tasso's *Discorsi del poema eroico*, first published in 1594, in which he suggests that the poet should place his action either in the remote past or in a distant land so that readers will be unable to question the accuracy of his presentation (Forcione 1970, 38; Riley 1962, 190). Montaigne similarly observes that

l'estrangeté mesme donne credit.... A cette cause, dict Platon, est-il bien plus aisé de satisfaire, parlant de la nature des Dieux, que de la nature des hommes, par ce que l'ignorance des auditeurs preste une belle et large carriere et toute liberté au maniement d'une matiere cachée. [1.32.215]

⟨strangeness itself lends credit.... For this reason, says Plato, it is much easier to give satisfaction when speaking of the nature of the gods than when speaking of the nature of men, because the ignorance of one's audience affords a fine broad range and full liberty in handling so obscure a subject. [Frame 1958, 159-60]⟩

Cervantes may also have placed Andrés' adventures in the exotic setting of a gypsy camp in order to let him demonstrate the flexibility in adapting to circumstances prized by so many Renaissance writers. Montaigne asserts:

Nostre principalle suffisance, c'est sçavoir s'appliquer à divers usages.... Les plus belles ames sont celles qui ont plus de variété et souplesse. [3.3.818]

⟨Our principal talent is the ability to apply ourselves to various practices.... The fairest souls are those that have the most variety and adaptability. [Frame 1958, 621]⟩

Castiglione's courtiers likewise consider the ability to adapt oneself to circumstances an essential requisite. Messer Federigo Fregoso stresses the importance of making sure all one's actions are appropriate to one's situation:

Voglio adunque che 'l nostro cortegiano . . . consideri
ben che cosa è quella che egli fa o dice e 'l loco dove la
fa, in presenzia di cui, a che tempo, la causa perché la
fa, la età sua, la professione, il fine dove tende e i mezzi
che a quello condur lo possono; e così con queste
avvertenzie s'accommodi discretamente a tutto quello
che fare o dir vole. [2.7.199-200]

⟨I would have our courtier . . . consider well what he
does or says, the place where he does it, in whose presence, its timeliness, the reason for doing it, his own
age, his profession, the end at which he aims, and the
means by which he can reach it; thus, keeping these
points in mind, let him act accordingly in whatever he
may choose to do or say. [Singleton 1959, 98]⟩

The perfect courtier, of course, will not allow his behavior
to be governed solely by circumstance. Andrés certainly
does not.

Andrés' unquestioning acceptance of the ethical code
that governs the behavior of the nobility is nowhere more
apparent than in the incident that leads to his imprison-
ment and thus indirectly to the discovery of Preciosa's true
identity. Falsely accused of theft by the innkeeper's daughter, whose proposal of marriage he has refused, Andrés is
abused by an arrogant soldier (un soldado bizarro), a
nephew of the mayor, who chances to be present:

—¿No veis cuál se ha quedado el gitanico podrido de
hurtar? . . . ¡Mirad si estuviera mejor este bellaco en
[las galeras], sirviendo a su Majestad, que no andarse
bailando de lugar en lugar y hurtando de venta en
monte! A fe de soldado que estoy por darle una bofe-
tada que le derribe a mis pies—. Y diciendo esto, sin
más ni más, alzó la mano y le dio un bofetón tal, que le
hizo volver de su embelesamiento y le hizo acordar que
no era Andrés Caballero, sino don Juan y caballero. Y
arremetiendo al soldado con mucha presteza y más có-

lera, le arrancó su misma espada y se la envainó en el cuerpo, dando con él muerto en tierra. [1:145]

⟨"Just look at this rotten thieving gypsy! ... This scoundrel ought to be serving his Majesty in the galleys instead of going from village to village dancing and stealing everything he can lay his hands on. On my honor as a soldier, I've a good mind to knock him down." And without another word he raised his hand and struck Andrés so hard that he came to his senses and remembered that he was not the gypsy Andrés Caballero but the nobleman Don Juan. He threw himself upon the soldier in a fit of anger and drawing the man's own sword from its scabbard ran him through, leaving him lying dead on the ground.⟩

The scene is shocking to modern readers, both because of the apparent casualness with which Andrés kills another man and because he is eventually allowed to go free with no punishment other than the payment of a sum to the dead man's family. Natalie Zemon Davis' study (1987) of sixteenth-century French letters of remission, by which a person accused of homicide appeals to the king for pardon, offers abundant evidence that Andres' action would not have shocked Cervantes' contemporaries. The paragraph quoted from *La gitanilla* clearly sets forth the extenuating circumstances. Andrés acts in what the French pardon tales call *chaude colle*, hot anger, which justifies the magistrate's decision to free him, though of course the magistrate also has other motives for doing so.

For Cervantes' contemporaries, moreover, Andrés' impulsive action, with no thought of the consequences, when he has been offended is proof not just of his innocence but of his nobility. It is the fact that Andrés finally turns out to be a nobleman and that he is to marry Preciosa, now revealed as the magistrate's long-lost daughter, that prompts her father to free him, as Cervantes makes clear. When the dead soldier's uncle learns that Andrés, now restored to his true identity as Don Juan de Cárcamo, is to marry Preciosa, he realizes he has lost any possibility of revenge: "el alcalde, tío del muerto, vio tomados los caminos de su venganza, pues no había de tener lugar el rigor de la justicia para ejecutarla en el yerno del Corregidor" (1:156).

The magistrate's action in freeing Andrés is hardly unusual. In England at this time Elizabeth I routinely gave "pardons of grace" to aristocratic murderers unless their crimes involved treason or public scandal (Lawrence Stone, cited in Davis 1987, 75). Cervantes, nevertheless, goes out of his way to suggest that Andrés is saved by a miracle. Preciosa urges the magistrate to postpone Andrés' execution, since Heaven may protect a person who has not sinned deliberately, "podrá ser que al que no pecó de malicia le enviase el cielo la salud de la gracia" (1:148), while the magistrate himself declares that only a miracle can account for so many coincidences: "tantas puntualidades juntas, ¿cómo podían suceder, si no fuera por milagro?" (1:150).

Timothy Hampton suggests that in *Don Quixote* Cervantes returns to "Montaigne's affirmation of an ethical model based on aristocratic values ... but only to reflect with melancholy on their vanity and their eclipse" (1990, 237). He asserts that "Cervantes depicts a world in which the imitation of models has run amok, but where the concern for virtue ... has virtually vanished" (ibid., 238). Hampton's statement is debatable with respect to *Don Quixote* and still more so with respect to the *Novelas ejemplares*. Frank Pierce has noted that "the flavour of the shorter tales is ... traditionalist and their emphasis that of a conservative believer in social values" (1953, 136; cf. Barrenechea 1961, 25-26; Clamurro 1989, 43). *La gitanilla* confirms Northrop Frye's remark that "one very obvious feature of romance is its pervasive social snobbery.... Sentimental romance gives us patterns of aristocratic courage and courtesy, and much of it adopts a 'blood will tell' convention, the association of moral virtue and social rank implied in the word 'noble.' A hero may appear to be of low social origin, but if he is a real hero he is likely to be revealed at the end of the story as belonging to the gentry" (1976, 161). The world of aristocratic privilege celebrated in sentimental romance shows signs of strain in *La gitanilla*, though they are less evident there than in *Don Quixote*, which Michael McKeon considers a precursor of the convergence of the destabilization of generic and social categories he believes resulted in the creation of the modern novel. By destabilization of social categories McKeon means the increased upward social mobility characteristic of early modern Europe and the consequent need to justify cases of evident disproportion between merit and status that stood in its way. He argues: "The notion of honor as a unity of outward circumstance and inward essence is the most fundamental justification for the hierarchical stratification of society. . . . It asserts . . . that the social order is not circumstantial and arbitrary, but corresponds to and expresses an analogous, intrinsic moral order. . . . [T]he romance convention of discovered parentage mediates the threat of noncorrespondence by problematically isolating physical beauty and true nobility apart from inherited nobility, only to reconfirm the wholeness of honor at the end of the story" (1987, 131-33).

McKeon believes that the ten years that separate the two parts of *Don Quixote* mark Cervantes' development from a progressive to a conservative ideology: "The Dorothea of Part I and the Don Quixote of Part II imply two distinct readings of the past and and two antithetical revolutionary programs for future social justice: the progressive utopianism of upward mobility and the career open to talents, and the conservative utopianism of the revival of harmonious 'feudal' social relations" (ibid., 287).

McKeon's claim that Cervantes had rejected conservative ideology by the time he came to write *Don Quixote* part 2 is questionable. As William H. Clamurro has noted, "the entire collection [of *Novelas ejemplares*] can . . . be viewed as a varied but essentially coherent set of lessons . . . that reflect a basically . . . conservative vision of social order" (1987, 40-41). The *Novelas ejemplares* offer little

evidence that Cervantes believed in either the possibility or
the desirability of upward social mobility, though he may of
course be expressing not his own political convictions but
those of his readers. The revelation that Preciosa's parents
are noble is accepted by everyone in the story as sufficient
explanation for the contrast between her appearance as a
gypsy and her insistence on behaving like a well-brought-up
young lady who refuses to listen to indecent language and
insists that the marriage bond must not be broken. Don
Juan de Cárcamo's lineage similarly accounts not only for
his fidelity to the ethical code of the nobility but also the
ease with which he surpasses the gypsies in their own sports
and pastimes. His ability to distinguish himself in the role
of the gypsy Andrés Caballero must have reassured Cervantes' aristocratic readers by confirming their sense of
their essential superiority, while the discovery of Preciosa's
true identity as Doña Costanza de Azevedo y de Meneses assured them of the essential rightness of the established social order.

Several of the *Novelas ejemplares,* including *La gitanilla,*
may be considered versions of pastoral (Hart 1981). Andrés'
stay among the gypsies is a variant of a theme found in
many Renaissance pastorals in which a courtier or group of
courtiers lives for a time among simple country people. Pastoral interludes of this kind afford the courtier an opportunity to try out an unfamiliar role, like the masquerades
discussed by Castiglione's Federico. They are a special case
of the eutrapelia Fray Juan Bautista Capataz found in the
Novelas ejemplares.

Cervantes offers his readers another version of pastoral in
La ilustre fregona. Preciosa's counterpart Costanza is
equally remarkable for her ability to remain true to the ideals of her own class while living amid the physical surroundings and moral confusion of a popular inn—an ability
symbolized by her Christian name, which incidentally she
shares with Preciosa, as we discover at the end of *La gitanilla* (1:149). Like Preciosa, Costanza is the daughter of no-

ble parents. She is an illegitimate child, secretly placed with the innkeeper and his wife to keep her parents' lives free from scandal. The innkeeper, of course, knows her real identity and gives her only tasks suitable to her real station in life: her sole duty is to keep the keys of the silver chest. She is a scullery maid who never enters the scullery, "una fregona que no friega."

The role given to Andrés in *La gitanilla* is assigned in *La ilustre fregona* to two young men, Diego de Carriazo and Tomás de Avendaño. When the story begins Carriazo has just returned from three years spent in the tunny fisheries of Andalusia. There, Cervantes tells us, many well-to-do fathers go to seek runaway sons attracted by the promise of a carefree life of adventure. Carriazo's life there shares more than one feature with the shepherd's life as it is presented in the pastoral tradition:

> Para él todos los tiempos del año le eran dulce y templada primavera; tan bien dormía en parvas como en colchones; con tanto gusto se soterraba en un pajar de un mesón como si se acostara entre dos sábanas de holanda. [3:45-46]

> ⟨For him every season was spring, sweet and mild; he slept as well on a heap of grain as in a featherbed; he buried himself in the hayloft of an inn with as much pleasure as if he were lying between linen sheets.⟩

Yet, despite the pleasure he finds in the life of a *pícaro*, Carriazo, like Andrés in *La gitanilla*, remains completely unsullied by his environment:

> Con serle anejo a este género de vida la miseria y estrecheza, mostraba Carriazo ser un príncipe en sus cosas: a tiro de escopeta, en mil señales, descubría ser bien nacido, porque era generoso y bien partido con sus camaradas. . . . En fin, en Carriazo vio el mundo un pícaro virtuoso, limpio, bien criado y más que medianamente discreto. [3:46-47]

⟨Although poverty and discomfort are inseparable
from this kind of life, Carriazo behaved like a prince;
even at a distance he revealed in all sorts of ways that
he was nobly born, for he was generous and liberal
with his companions. . . . In short, Carriazo proved a
virtuous rogue, clean, well bred, and more sensible
than most people.⟩

To readers familiar with Mateo Alemán's picaresque novel
Guzmán de Alfarache, then at the height of its popularity,
the phrase "un pícaro virtuoso" must have seemed as much
an oxymoron as Cervantes' title *La ilustre fregona*.

Both *La gitanilla* and *La ilustre fregona* may be seen in
terms of the traditional comic plot in which a young man of
the upper classes falls in love with a slave girl or an apparent
prostitute. Why did Cervantes include two stories so much
alike in his *Novelas ejemplares*? Publishers then usually is-
sued collection of stories or plays in groups of twelve; perhaps he simply used whatever he had on hand to make up
the required number (McKendrick 1980, 274-75). Perhaps,
however, the similarity between the two stories is inten-
tional and meant to be noticed by the reader.

For Roman Jakobson, the essence of poetry is "recurrent
returns" (1987, 145), a special case of his principle that "the
poetic function projects the principle of equivalence from
the axis of selection into the axis of contiguity" (ibid., 71). In
parallelistic verse, for example, the repetition may bring out
the similarity between apparently dissimilar statements;
the second occurrence may "give us the clue for the construction of the first" (ibid., 148, quoting P. A. Boodberg). In
narrative, too, the return of an incident may make us mod-
ify or reject our initial interpretation of it.

I have suggested elsewhere that Cervantes may have bor-
rowed from Ariosto his practice of repeating an incident
with different characters. Two characters placed in similar
situations may behave either in the same way or in radically
different ways. In both cases, the repetition of the episode
constitutes an important part of its meaning (Hart 1989, 24-

25). The challenge to the reader, in the absence of any explicit comment by the narrator, is to determine in what sense the two episodes are similar. As Gérard Genette observes, "The 'repetition' is in fact a mental construction, which eliminates from each occurrence everything belonging to it that is peculiar to itself, in order to preserve only what it shares with all the others of the same class. . . . What we will name here 'identical events' or 'recurrence of the same event' is a series of several similar events *considered only in terms of their resemblance"* (1980, 113). In Genette's terms we can say that Cervantes narrates a single action both once and more than once: once in the sense that *La gitanilla* and *La ilustre fregona* differ greatly in detail and more than once in the sense that both novellas belong to the same general category.

If we consider *La gitanilla* and *La ilustre fregona* not as individual "versions of pastoral" but as parts of the collection *Novelas ejemplares,* we may see them as exemplifying the device some contemporary critics refer to as a *mise en abyme.* Lucien Dällenbach defines it as "any aspect enclosed within a work that shows a similarity with the work that contains it" and says that "its essential property is that it brings out the meaning and form of the work" (1989, 8; cf. Neuschäfer 1990).

John Lyons observes that the repetition of an incident is what enables the reader to identify it as an example: "In describing example in general only the relation between generalization and specific instance is essential, and this relation is an interpretive one. Unless the reader realizes that the instance is given to represent or support a broader statement, the reader cannot recognize example" (1989, 23). Our willingness to interpret an episode as a *mise en abyme* depends on our willingness to agree that it fulfills Lyons' definition of an example, "a dependent statement qualifying a more general and independent statement." The latter is, of course, the meaning of the work as a whole.

What kind of general statement do our two novellas qualify? I noted in Chapter 1 that Cervantes did not necessarily expect all of his readers to interpret his stories in the same way, though he would certainly have rejected some interpretations as inappropriate. Among those that might have occurred to a contemporary reader of *La gitanilla* and *La ilustre fregona* are such maxims as blood will tell, which might have proved especially attractive to the noblemen who formed an important part of the public that bought works of fiction. A less aristocratic reader might have preferred to see the two novellas as exemplifying the maxim that virtue is always rewarded. Neither of these interpretations excludes the other. A single reader, on rereading or recalling the novella, might favor now one, now the other. And of course these two interpretations represent only a tiny sample of those that might have occurred to individual readers and that would have been accepted as legitimate.

Cervantes' contemporaries expected works of literature to be arguments about something, generally a moral or philosophical truth, but they did not limit themselves to trying to discover the argument that had served the author as a point of departure (Wallace 1974, 276). Their attitude is summed up in Montaigne's assertion in "Of the Education of Children":

> J'ay leu en Tite Live cent choses que tel n'y a pas leu, Plutarque en y a leu cent, outre ce que j'y ay sceu lire, et, à l'adventure, outre ce que l'autheur y avoit mis. [1.26.156]

> ⟨I have read in Livy a hundred things that another man has not read in him, Plutarch has read a hundred besides the ones I could read, and perhaps besides what the author himself had put in. [Frame 1958, 115]⟩

CHAPTER 3

Vying with Heliodorus:
El amante liberal

El amante liberal has found little favor with modern readers; Peter Dunn calls it "the least attractive" of the *Novelas
ejemplares* (1973, 93). Rodríguez Marín did not include it in
the selection he edited for the Clásicos Castellanos in 1914;
both Harriet de Onís and C. A. Jones omit it from their
translations of selected *novelas*. Seventeenth-century readers felt very differently. James Mabbe thought well enough
of *El amante liberal* to include it among the six novellas
he translated for English readers in 1640. The translations
and adaptations of the *Novelas ejemplares* offered to
seventeenth-century French and English readers suggest
that they preferred the more aristocratic novellas, like *La española inglesa* and *El amante liberal*, whose protagonists
are noblemen and their ladies, to those whose protagonists
are juvenile delinquents (*Rinconete y Cortadillo*) or dogs (*El
coloquio de los perros*). Cervantes' Spanish contemporaries
probably felt the same way.

   While it is easy to show that *El amante liberal* was more
popular in the seventeenth century than it is today, it is
harder to determine the nature of its appeal for Cervantes'
contemporaries. The dedicatory verses by several of his
friends that precede the text in the first edition of the
Novelas ejemplares presumably stress qualities in the stories that the author himself wanted to see emphasized. The
verses are, however, too vague to be of much help. More useful are the several *aprobaciones*, in particular that by another friend, the Trinitarian friar Juan Bautista Capataz.

   In stressing what he calls "la verdadera eutropelia" to be

found in the novellas Fray Juan Bautista returns to a point
made by the French humanist Jacques Amyot in the prologue to his translation of Heliodorus's *Ethiopian History*
(Paris, 1547). Amyot's prologue is included in the Spanish
translation by an anonymous "secreto amigo de su patria"
published in Antwerp in 1554 (Forcione 1970, 20). In the prologue Amyot declares:

> La imbecilidad de nuestra natura no puede sufrir que el
> entendimiento esté siempre ocupado a leer materias
> graves y verdaderas, no más que el cuerpo no podría du-
> rar sin intermisión al trabajo de muchas obras. Por lo
> cual, es menester algunas veces, cuando nuestro espíri-
> tu está turbado de algunos infortunios, o cansado de
> mucho estudio, usar de algunos pasatiempos para le
> apartar de tristes pensamientos y imaginaciones, o, a
> lo menos, usar de algún descanso y alivio para le tornar
> después a poner más alegre y vivo en la consideración
> y contemplación de las cosas de más importancia. [He-
> liodorus 1954, lxxvii-lxxviii]

> ⟨The weakness of our nature cannot bear for our under-
> standing always to be concerned with grave and true
> matters, any more than our bodies can perform many
> tasks without rest. For this reason, it is sometimes
> necessary, when we are troubled by misfortune or ex-
> hausted by much study, to take up some pastime in
> order to drive away melancholy thoughts and imagin-
> ings, or at least to give ourselves some rest and relief so
> that we will be more cheerful and better able to con-
> sider more important things.⟩

Cervantes may have been familiar with Amyot's prologue;
he certainly knew Heliodorus's romance, though perhaps in
an edition that omits the prologue. He declares in the prologue to the *Novelas ejemplares* that he hopes to live long
enough to complete *The Trials of Persiles and Sigismunda*,
a work he says dares to compete with Heliodorus: "Tras
ellas [las *Novelas*], si la vida no me deja, te ofrezco los *Tra-*

bajos de Persiles, libro que se atreve a competir con Heliodoro" (1:65). In fact, several of the *Novelas ejemplares* dare to compete with the *Ethiopian History,* none more obviously than *El amante liberal,* perhaps the closest of the twelve to the kind of romance Spanish critics misleadingly call the Byzantine novel. Diana de Armas Wilson is fully justified in stressing that even in *Don Quixote* Cervantes does not reject romance but only some features peculiar to chivalric romance (1991, 29).

There are a number of sixteenth- and seventeenth-century responses to the *Ethiopian History* that, like Amyot's preface, enable us to infer a good deal about the way Cervantes' contemporaries responded to *El amante liberal.* Amyot considers the *Ethiopian History* a profoundly moral work:

Demás de la ingeniosa ficción, hay en algunos lugares hermosos discursos sacados de la filosofía natural y moral, muchos dichos notables y palabras sentenciosas, muchas oraciones y pláticas, en los cuales el artificio de elocuencia está muy bien empleado, y en toda ella las pasiones y afecciones humanas, pintadas tan al verdadero y con tan gran honestidad, que no se podrá sacar ocasión de malhacer. Porque de todas aficiones ilícitas y deshonestas, él hace el fin desdichado; y, al contrario, de las buenas y honestas, dichoso. [Heliodorus 1954, lxxx].

⟨In addition to the ingenious fiction there are in it fine discourses drawn from natural and moral philosophy, many noteworthy sayings and maxims, many speeches and dialogues in which the artifice of eloquence is very skillfully handled and in the whole work passions and human desires are treated so truthfully and yet with such decency that they cannot lead anyone to behave immorally. For the author makes all illicit and dishonest passions end in disaster and on the contrary makes good and honest ones end happily.⟩

Many sixteenth-century Spanish writers shared Amyot's view that the *Ethiopian History* was a morally exemplary text (Bataillon 1950, 2:222-25; Vilanova 1949, 124). English writers, too, praised the *Ethiopian History* for its moral teaching. Thomas Underdowne, for example, in the note "To the Reader" prefixed to his translation (London, 1606), declares: "If I shall compare it with other of like argument, I thinke none cometh neere it. . . . This booke punisheth the faults of evil doers, and rewardeth the well livers. What a king is *Hydaspes*? What a patterne of a good prince? . . . What a lewde woman was *Arsace*? What a patern of evill behavior?" (quoted in Lanham 1965, 388). Like Oscar Wilde's Miss Prism in *The Importance of Being Earnest*, sixteenth-century readers believed that in a properly organized story, "the good [end] happily, and the bad unhappily. That is what Fiction means."

To see the *Ethiopian History* as a morally exemplary text goes counter to the view of the Greek romances held by many scholars. In his study of Sir Philip Sidney's *Old Arcadia*, Richard Lanham cites with approval some remarks on the amorality of the Greek romances in Samuel Lee Wolff's *The Greek Romances in Elizabethan Prose Fiction* (1912) and asserts: "The Greek romance was an essentially trivial genre, evoking a shallow emotional response by a combination of melodrama and rhetorical display. Clever though it may have been, it was 'entertainment' in the worst sense of the word. . . . It would be doing Sidney an injustice to fit this noose to the neck of the Old *Arcadia*. For, taking over the basic techniques of rhetorical fiction, Sidney infused them with a strict, pervasive moral consciousness. . . . Sidney has moralized Heliodorus" (1965, 385-86). It is most unlikely, however, that Sidney saw himself as adding a moral content to a fundamentally amoral fiction. Sixteenth-century readers certainly did not believe that Heliodorus's work was amoral, as Amyot makes clear in the prologue to his translation.

Amyot asserts that the aim of fiction is to produce wonder (*admiración*) and the delight that comes from strange and wonderful things (*cosas extrañas y llenas de admira-*

ción) (Heliodorus 1954, lxxix). The qualities that produce admiración are concisely set forth in the *Tablas poéticas* (1617) of Francisco Cascales, which Cervantes may have read in manuscript (Riley 1962, 4-5). Whether he read it or not is not really very important, since Cascales' treatise is largely a restatement of the work of the sixteenth-century Italian preceptists who attempted a fusion of Horatian and Aristotelian principles.

According to Cascales, admiración may be produced by things, by words, and by the order and variety with which both are presented to the reader: "La admiración nace de las cosas, de las palabras, de la orden y de la variedad" (1975, 170). By "things" Cascales means the incidents of the plot. The "coincidences of capture, voyage and reunion" (Lowe 1970-71, 400) that fill the pages of the *Ethiopian History* and of *El amante liberal* awaken the reader's wonder because they are not everyday occurrences. But while the incidents of the plot may suffice to make the reader feel admiración, they will do so much more effectively if the writer knows how to show them to advantage. Admiración may be produced not just by the actions of the characters but by the order and variety with which they are narrated, that is, by what we should call "narrative devices."

Amyot's prologue shows clearly both that sixteenth-century readers were attentive to the use of such narrative techniques and that they considered them a cause of the admiración that is the proper aim of fiction. He praises the *Ethiopian History* because Heliodorus chose to begin it *in medias res*:

Y cierto la disposición es singular, porque comienza en la mitad de la Historia, como hacen los poetas heroicos, lo cual causa, de *prima facie*, una grande admiración a los lectores, y les engendra un apasionado deseo de oír y entender el comienzo, y todavía los atrae también con la ingeniosa lección de su cuento, que no entienden lo que han leído en el comienzo del primer libro, hasta que veen el fin del quinto; y cuando allí han llegado, aún les queda mayor deseo de ver el fin, que antes tenían de ver el principio. De suerte que siempre el entendimiento queda suspenso hasta que viene a la conclusión, lo cual deja el lector satisfecho, como lo son aquellos que al fin vienen a gozar de una cosa muy deseada y de mucho tiempo esperada. [Heliodorus 1954, lxxx-lxxxi]

⟨Certainly its arrangement is striking, because the author begins in the middle of the story, as the epic poets do, which immediately arouses great wonder [*admiración*] in the readers and gives them a passionate desire to know and understand the beginning and also attracts them with the ingenious structure of his narrative, since they will not understand what they have read in the beginning of book 1 until they have reached the end of book 5; and when they do reach it they will desire even more strongly to know the ending than they did to know the beginning. Thus the understanding is kept in a state of tension until the end, which gives the reader the satisfaction felt by those who come at last to enjoy something greatly desired and long hoped for.⟩

Amyot's stress on the role of narrative techniques in producing admiración helps to explain why, as Keith Whinnom observes, "It is difficult to think of any narrative device with which Spanish writers of the late fifteenth and the sixteenth centuries did not at some time play" (1982, 255).

Cascales insists that admiración may be produced not just by the incidents of the plot and their arrangement but by the very words used to tell the story. The language must be dignified and sententious and adorned with splendid rhetorical figures: "Las palabras serán maravillosas que son escogidas con grande juizio, sentenciosas, graves, de dulce son, con galanas figuras de la elocuencia" (1975, 171). Cervantes surely expected his readers to admire the elaborate rhetoric of a long speech like the one in which Ricardo tells his friend the renegade Mahamut how he was captured by Turks. Ricardo has just explained that he had learned that Leonisa and his rival Cornelio were attending a party in the garden of Cornelio's father:

—Súpelo—replicó Ricardo—, y al mismo tiempo que lo supe me ocupó el alma una furia, una rabia y un infierno de celos, con tanta vehemencia y rigor, que me sacó de mis sentidos, como lo verás por lo que luego hice, que fue irme al jardín donde me dijeron que estaban, y hallé a la más de la gente solazándose, y debajo de un nogal sentados a Cornelio y a Leonisa, aunque desviados un poco. Cuál ellos quedaron de mi vista, no lo sé; de mí sé decir que quedé tal con la suya, que perdí la de mis ojos, y me quedé como estatua sin voz ni movimiento alguno. Pero no tardó mucho en despertar el enojo a la cólera, y la cólera a la sangre del corazón, y la sangre a la ira, y la ira a las manos y a la lengua; puesto que las manos se ataron con el respeto a mi parecer debido al hermoso rostro que tenía delante. Pero la lengua rompió el silencio con estas razones: "Contenta estarás, ¡oh enemiga mortal de mi descanso!, en tener con tanto sosiego delante de tus ojos la causa que hará que los míos vivan en perpetuo y doloroso llanto. Llégate, llégate, cruel, un poco más, y enrede tu yedra a ese inútil tronco que te busca; peina o ensortija aquellos cabellos de ese tu nuevo Ganimedes, que tibiamente te solicita.... ¿Piensas, por ventura, soberbia y mal considerada doncella, que contigo sola se han de romper y faltar las leyes y fueros que en semejantes casos en el mundo se usan? ¿Piensas, quiero decir, que este mozo, altivo por su riqueza, arrogante por su gallardía, inexperto por su edad poca, confiado por su linaje, ha de querer, ni poder, ni saber guardar firmeza en sus amores, ni estimar lo inestimable, ni conocer lo que conocen los maduros y experimentados años? No lo pienses, si lo piensas, porque no tiene otra cosa buena el mundo, sino hacer sus

acciones siempre de una misma manera, por que no se
engañe nadie sino por su propia ignorancia. En los pocos años está la inconstancia mucha; en los ricos, la
soberbia; la vanidad, en los arrogantes, y en los hermosos, el desdén, y en los que todo esto tienen, la
necedad, que es madre de todo mal suceso. [1:167-69]

James Mabbe's English version captures much of the rhetorical force of Ricardo's speech:

I knew that (replied Ricardo) and in that very instant
that I knew it, my soule was possessed with such a
fury, such a rage, and such a hell of jealousies, and with
that vehemencie and rigour, that it bereaved mee of my
senses, as thou shalt plainely, by that which I presently
did see, which was this.

I hyed mee to the Garden where I was told they
were, where I found most of the company solasing
themselves, and *Cornelio* & *Leonisa* sitting under a
Walnut-tree, somewhat out of the way from the rest.
How my sight pleased them I doe not know, but know,
to say so much of my selfe, that her sight wrought so
upon mee, that I lost the sight of mine owne eyes; and
stood stocke still like a *Statua*, without either voice, or
motion. But I continued not long so, before that my anger awakened my choler, choler, heated my bloud; my
bloud, inflamed rage; and rage gave motion to my
hands, and tongue. Howbeit my hands were bound by
the respect which (me'thought) was due to that fayre
face which I had before mee; But my tongue breaking
silence, vented forth these words:

How canst thou finde in thy heart, how give thy
selfe content (Oh thou mortall enemie of my rest) in
having, (and therin taking so much pleasure) before
thine eyes, the cause which must make mine to over-
flow with rivers of teares; and by my continuall weep-
ing, become another Deluge? Come, come, (cruell as
thou art) a little nearer, and wreathe thy twining Ivie,

about this unprofitable truncke, which wooes thy em-
bracings. Let him lay his head in thy lap, and let thy
fingers learne to play with those breaded lockes of this
thy new *Ganimede*. . . . Thinkest thou peradventure
(thou proud and ill advised Damosell) that this young
Princoxe, presumptuous by reason of his riches; arrogant, by your gracing of him, unexperienced, in that
hee is too young; and insolent by his relying on his Lin-
age, will love as he ought, and you deserve? No, hee
cannot, no, hee knowes not how to love constantly;
nor to esteeme that which is inestimable, nor come to
have that understanding and knowledge, which accom-
panies ripe and experimented yeares. If you thinke so,
do not thinke it; for the World hath no other good
thing, save the doing of its actions alwaies after one
and the same manner. For none are deceived, but by
their owne ignorance: In yong men there is much in-
constancie; in rich, pride; vanitie in the arrogant; in
the beautifull, disdaine; and in those that have all
these, foolishnesse, which is the mother of all ill suc-
cesse. [Cervantes 1928, 134-36]

Many of Cervantes' contemporaries would have had no difficulty in identifying the rhetorical figures that Cervantes
introduces into Ricardo's speech and that Mabbe faithfully
reproduces in his English version. Their schooling would
have provided endless drill in doing precisely that (Vickers
1988, 259-61). They would have appreciated Ricardo's fond-
ness for amplification by synonyms (una *furia*, una *rabia* y
un *infierno de celos, romper* y *faltar* las *leyes* y *fueros*). He
is also fond of erotesis or interrogatio, that is, of asking rhetorical questions whose answer is clearly implied, here
combined with anaphora (¿*Piensas*...? ¿*Piensas*, quiero decir . . . ?) and followed by a combination of dehortatio, advice to the contrary, and polyptoton, the use of different
forms of the same word (No lo *pienses*, si lo *piensas*). Polyptoton also figures prominently in the preceding sentence (*estimar* lo *inestimable, conocer* lo que *conocen*), which is

marked also by an elaborate use of synonymia and of isocolon, repetition of phrases of the same length and similar structure (altivo por su riqueza, arrogante por su gallardía, confiado por su linaje). Ricardo uses personification to suggest that his actions were carried out without conscious intention. His skillful use of anadiplosis, the repetition of a word from the end of one phrase to begin the next, suggests the speed with which his emotions led to actions: "no tardó mucho en despertar el enojo a la *cólera,* y la *cólera* a la *sangre* del corazón, y la *sangre* a la *ira,* y la *ira* a las *manos* y a la *lengua;* puesto que las *manos* se ataron con el respeto a mi parecer debido al hermoso rostro que tenía delante. Pero la *lengua* rompió el silencio. . . ." The figure seems to have been a favorite with Cervantes; he uses it in his account of the fight at the inn in *Don Quixote:*

> Y así como suele decirse: el gato al *rato,* el *rato* a la *cuerda,* la *cuerda* al palo, daba el arriero a *Sancho, Sancho* a la *moza,* la *moza* a él, el ventero a la *moza,* y todos menudeaban con tanta priesa, que no se daban punto de reposo. . . . [1.16.205]
>
> ⟨And so as the saying goes, the cat beat the rat, the rat beat the rope, the rope beat the stick, the muledriver beat Sancho, Sancho the maid, the maid beat him, the innkeeper the maid, and all pounded away at a great rate without a moment's rest.⟩

In this passage, the tone is of course very different, in part because the rhetorical figure forms part of the narrative and is not attributed to a character, as it is in *El amante liberal.* The artificiality of Ricardo's discourse is heightened by the fact that a substantial portion of it, which begins with the words "Contenta estarás," is a quotation within a quotation, in which Ricardo claims he is repeating the exact words he had used one year, three days, and five hours before, "de hoy hace un año, tres días y cinco horas" (1:167).

Twentieth-century readers tend to dislike speeches of this kind. Francisco A. de Icaza, for example, charges that in *El*

amante liberal "there is an excess of rhetoric . . . that bor-
ders on the comic, and that perhaps made Cervantes himself laugh" (quoted in Amezúa 1956-58, 2:58-59). Juan
Bautista Avalle-Arce similarly objects that Leocadia's
highly rhetorical speech on discovering that she has been
raped by Rodolfo in *La fuerza de la sangre* is "completely
implausible" (Cervantes 1982, 2:27). Cervantes' contemporaries felt very differently. Though Spaniards were famous
all over Europe for their extravagant speech, delight in rhetorical display was not confined to Spain. James Mabbe's
translation of *El amante liberal* faithfully preserves and occasionally even heightens the rhetorical features found in
Cervantes' text. Ian Watt defines the attitude of seventeenth-
-century readers very well when he says that before the rise
of the novel as the dominant form of prose fiction "the implicit assumption of educated writers and critics was that an
author's skill was shown, not in the closeness with which
he made his words correspond to their objects, but in the literary sensitivity with which his style reflected the linguistic decorum appropriate to its subject" (1957, 28-29).
"Linguistic decorum" does not mean the way real people
talk in similar circumstances but rather the way writers
customarily represent their characters as speaking. William
Nelson notes that many prefaces and dedications to works
of Renaissance fiction "dismiss story itself as merely delightful and direct attention to the substance which justifies
it. The discerning reader . . . is given to understand that the
narrative was designed to provide opportunity for moral and
philosophical discourses, model speeches and letters, sententious comment, descriptions, witty repartee, rhetorical
displays, information about strange lands and ancient
times, and other matter useful or worthy of admiration"
(1973, 60). Amyot does this in the passage already quoted
where he praises the *Ethiopian History* for its "hermosos
discursos sacados de la filosofía natural y moral." Peter Hey-
lyn, in his *Microcosmus* (1620), similarly asserts that Heliodorus's novel is "a book which beside its excellent
language, rare contrivances, and delectable studies, hath in

it all the strains of Poesy, comprehendeth the universal art
of speaking, and to them that can discerne and will observe,
notable rules for demeanour both private and publike"
(quoted in Watt 1982, 199).

Sixteenth-century readers felt free to divide up a text in this
way because the kind of moral benefit they expected to derive from their reading was unlike anything a modern reader
is likely to look for. The annotated editions in which *Orlando furioso* was read throughout the sixteenth century
show clearly that the commentators' assumptions about the
nature of their task were quite different from those of modern critics. The commentators do not attempt to describe an
ideal reader's total response to a text, nor do they try to demonstrate the relationship between the whole work and each
of its parts. They try instead to single out elements in the
text that can serve as a springboard for further reflection,
usually on moral or philosophical questions, in order to
demonstrate the moral benefit the reader may gain by con-
templating the parts singly and applying the lessons he
learns to the circumstances of his own life (Hart 1989,
115-16).

In discussing *La gitanilla*, I noted Tasso's insistence that
the poet will do well to give his story a setting so remote in
time or space or both that his readers will be unable to question his account. Alonso López Pinciano, whose *Philoso-
phia poética antigua* (1596) Cervantes probably knew,
praises Heliodorus for setting his story in Ethiopia, a country about which his Greek readers knew too little to contra-
dict what he says about it (Forcione 1970, 79-81). Cervantes
may have chosen Cyprus for the setting of the principal action of *El amante liberal* for similar reasons. Few contemporary readers of the *Novelas ejemplares* would have had
firsthand experience of life in Turkish-occupied Cyprus.
Neither did Cervantes, though in describing it he could
draw on his experience as a captive in Algiers.

If Cyprus was unfamiliar territory to most of Cervantes'
readers, and indeed to Cervantes himself, the Turkish pres-

ence in the Mediterranean was a matter of immediate concern to them. The raids conducted by North African corsairs had a profound psychological effect, which was not limited to the coastal areas where such attacks were most frequent. As Ellen G. Friedman notes, the fear created by the raids "can be compared with modern urban crime, in that the actual number of victims is relatively small, but society as a whole is terrorized" (1983, 165). The scene in which Ricardo and Leonisa are seized by Turkish corsairs transfers to Sicily a scene all too familiar to seventeenth-century Spaniards.

This topical quality differentiates *El amante liberal* from the *Ethiopian History*. Mikhail Bakhtin's illuminating discussion of the Greek romances reveals the distance that separates Cervantes' novella from Heliodorus. The Greek romances, according to Bakhtin, make no reference to the real world of space and time. They are wholly unconcerned with history: "No matter where we go in the world of the Greek romance, with all its countries and cities, its buildings and works of art, there are absolutely no indications of historical time, no identifying traces of the era" (1981, 91). Geographical space receives no more attention than historical time: "The world of the Greek romance is an *alien world.* . . . Its heroes are there for the first time; they have no organic ties or relationships with it; the laws governing the sociopolitical and everyday life of this world are foreign to them. . . . But in the Greek romance the alien quality of this world is not emphasized and we cannot therefore call it exotic. Exoticism presupposes a deliberate *opposition of what is alien to what is one's own*, the otherness of what is foreign is emphasized, savored, as it were. . . . There is none of this in the Greek romance" (1981, 101). By contrast, Cervantes constantly stresses the strangeness of the Turkish world in which Ricardo and Leonisa find themselves.

Cervantes has been praised for his tolerance toward the Turks in *El amante liberal*. While it is true that the narrator praises the Turkish judicial system for its reliance on common sense rather than on legal technicalities and for the speed with which cases are resolved (1:181), he does so in order to justify an important point in the plot: the cadi's ability to decide on the spot who will be allowed to buy Leonisa from the Jew who acquired her after the shipwreck that took the life of her Turkish captor.

Cervantes' treatment of the Turks stresses the moral superiority of Christians over Moslems by turning his principal Turkish characters into buffoons. The comedy in *El amante liberal* is centered on the *cadi* and his wife, whose adventures form a comic subplot that, as often in the Spanish theater of the Golden Age, parallels the serious main plot centered on Ricardo and Leonisa. Cervantes may have chosen to treat the cadi as a comic figure partly in order to reassure his readers that the Turk is too absurd to be taken seriously as a threat to the principal characters. The eagerness with which the cadi accepts the advice of his slaves Ricardo and Mahamut serves effectively to allay the reader's fears for the success of Ricardo's plan to rescue Leonisa in much the same way that in *Rinconete y Cortadillo* Rinconete's boldness in mocking Monipodio's malapropisms shows that, despite Monipodio's frightening appearance he is not really to be feared, at least by those clever enough to know how to deal with him.

Concern with the real world of contemporary Europe likewise separates *El amante liberal* from the medieval romances that developed into the romances of chivalry Cervantes parodies in *Don Quixote*. As Erich Auerbach observes, "Courtly culture gives rise to the idea, which long remained a factor of considerable importance in Europe, that nobility, greatness, and intrinsic values have nothing in common with everyday reality" (1953, 139). In *El amante liberal* Cervantes not only emphasizes the moral teaching implicit in the *Ethiopian History*, or at least in sixteenth-century interpretations of it, but moves the setting closer to the real world of his readers. The two points are of course connected, as Richard Lanham notes with reference to Sidney's *Arcadia*: "Arcadia is not a fairyland [;] its strongest ties are with the England of Sidney's day. . . . The Old *Arcadia* shows that nobility—rightly construed—has a great deal to do with everyday reality, that the nobility which neglects the real world is a radically tarnished one" (1965, 388). The "realism" of *El amante liberal*, like the much more attenuated "realism" of Sidney's *Arcadia*, makes a moral point.

It is the nature of this moral point that marks the clearest difference between Cervantes' novella and Heliodorus's romance. We have noted that Cervantes' contemporaries believed that the *Ethiopian History* provides examples both of virtuous persons who are to be imitated and of evil ones who serve as *exempla vitandi*. Heliodorus does not, however, show how character may be transformed as a result of experience, as most modern novelists do. The process is neatly symbolized in the well-known formula that Arthur Danto (1965, 236) proposes as the basic structure of all narratives: an event (H) brings about a transformation (F → G) in a subject (x) over the course of time $(t_1 \rightarrow t_2 \rightarrow t_3)$:

1) x is F at t_1
2) H happens to x at t_2
3) x is G at t_3.

The events of Heliodorus's narrative occur in what Bakhtin calls "adventure time," in which the series of events narrated is in principle both reversible, since the events leave no mark on the characters, and infinite, since new adventures may be added at any point (1981, 87-110). The world of *El amante liberal*—in Bakhtin's terminology, its chronotope—is quite different. It is the world of the Baroque novel, in which "everything . . . is a touchstone, a means for testing all the sides and qualities of the hero" (ibid, 388). The Ricardo who recognizes at the end of the novella that he has no right to demand that Leonisa return his love for her is no longer the self-centered and headstrong young man he was when the story began.

CHAPTER 4

Double-Voiced Discourse: *Rinconete y Cortadillo*

In *Rinconete y Cortadillo* Cervantes once more places the action in an unfamiliar setting. This time the setting is the underworld of Seville, then the largest city in Spain and one of the largest in Europe, with a population of about 150,000, "a city whose streets, at least in the popular imagination, were paved with the gold and silver of the Indies.... [But] its wealth was inevitably distributed with extreme inequality—nowhere in Spain were the social contrasts starker. An affluent elite ... indulged spectacularly in conspicuous consumption. But there was also a vast, poverty-stricken sub-world of unemployed and underemployed—vagabonds, rogues, street-urchins, casual labourers, dock-workers, hawkers, pedlars, water-sellers, all of them anxiously wondering where and how to get a square meal" (Elliott 1989, 272-73). Cervantes lived in Seville from 1596 to 1602. In *El coloquio de los perros* the dog Berganza calls the city a shelter for the poor and a refuge for the outcast, "amparo de pobres y refugio de desechados" (3:259). It was hardly that for Cervantes. In 1597 he was committed to the royal prison in Seville for alleged discrepancies in the sums he had reported receiving as a tax collector. There he spent seven months, "surrounded by pickpockets, confidence tricksters, prostitutes, and murderers: a splendid source of information about the Sevillian underworld, which [he] was to make full use of in *Rinconete and Cortadillo* and *The Dogs' Colloquy*" (McKendrick 1980, 174-75). Just how much use he made of it is open to question. Ruth Pike notes that "we know very little about the *gente del hampa*, or underworld, for available sources are few and incomplete. Judicial records are practically nonexistent and the notarial deeds, the source of so much information on the social life of Seville, are silent on such marginal and transient beings whose style of life and meager possessions did not require formal recording" (1972, 193). Pike's account of the Seville underworld is based largely on literary sources, including several works by Cervantes. Mary Elizabeth Perry similarly uses *Rinconete y Cortadillo* as a source for her account of criminal activity in early modern Seville (1980).

Few of Cervantes' contemporaries, unlike Cervantes himself, would have had firsthand experience of the Seville underworld. Most of them were probably not much interested in the accuracy of his portrayal in *Rinconete y Cortadillo*. At best they might have conceded that the scene he describes might have some counterpart in reality, as some readers of the novels of Len Deighton and John Le Carré accept their accounts of the way spies operate as plausible, if not necessarily accurate. The interest of Cervantes' contemporaries in *Rinconete y Cortadillo* probably lay in the novella's capacity for provoking admiratio through its exotic setting and grotesque characters.

The strangeness of the setting in *Rinconete y Cortadillo* is emphasized by the fact that we see it through the eyes of two newcomers who freely express the admiratio they feel on witnessing their new surroundings. For the first time in the *Novelas ejemplares*, however, the principal characters are not drawn from the nobility. Rinconete's father is a *buldero*, a seller of indulgences; Cortadillo's is a tailor. Neither profession had much prestige; both were frequently the butt of jokes. It was perhaps partly for this reason that Cervantes did not place *Rinconete y Cortadillo* at the beginning of his collection of novellas. His contemporaries often equated the aesthetic prestige of a literary work with the social prestige of its principal characters (Riley 1962, 132-33). Characters of inferior social status were then generally confined to comic works or to comic, and therefore minor, roles in serious ones. A. A. Parker is surely right in asserting that in *Don*

Quixote Cervantes, like "the best of the Spanish picaresque novelists [was] engaged in breaking down the barrier between the comic and the serious" (1967, 26), and the assertion is equally true of the *Novelas ejemplares*. Cervantes' more thoughtful readers must have realized he was attempting to do precisely that, but such readers probably formed only a small part of his intended audience. Even for them *Rinconete y Cortadillo* probably seemed funnier than it does to some twentieth-century readers, who see the novella as an exposure of the horrors of life at the bottom of the social hierarchy.

Rinconete y Cortadillo begins with a detailed description of the boys' wretched appearance when they first meet: their clothes are an ill-matched assortment of odds and ends, their shoes in shreds, their hands and nails filthy. But when the boys introduce themselves to one another they speak as if they were not tramps but noblemen:

> —¿De qué tierra es vuesa merced, señor gentilhombre, y para adónde bueno camina?
> —Mi tierra, señor caballero—respondió el preguntado
> —, no la sé, ni para dónde camino, tampoco.
> —Pues en verdad—dijo el mayor—que no parece vuesa merced del cielo. [1:220]

> ⟨"What part of the country do you hail from, noble sir, and whither are you bound?"
> "My country, sir knight, " answered the other, "I know not, nor do I know where I am headed."
> "In truth," said the older of the two, "you don't look as if you had dropped from heaven."⟩

After they have told each other about themselves and how they come to be at the inn where they meet, Rinconete, the older, suggests that there is no point in keeping up the pretense that they are gentlemen:

> pues ya nos conocemos, no hay por qué aquesas grandezas ni altiveces: confesemos llanamente que no teníamos blanca, ni aún zapatos. [1:224]

〈"Now that we know each other, there is no point in putting on airs; let's confess plainly that we haven't a penny nor even a pair of shoes."〉

His new companion willingly agrees, but his answer is in the same elevated style as before:

—Sea así—respondió Diego Cortado, que así dijo el menor que se llamaba—: y pues nuestra amistad, como vuesa merced, señor Rincón, ha dicho, ha de ser per-petua, comencémosla con santas y loables ceremonias. [1:225]

〈"Agreed," answered Diego Cortado, for that was what the younger boy said his name was, "and since our friendship, as you, Mister Rincón, have said, is to be for life, let us begin it with holy and praiseworthy ceremonies."〉

Neither boy attempts to deceive the other by his way of speaking. They are not trying to hide a sordid reality but amusing themselves by playing with language.

Soon after their arrival in Seville Rinconete and Corta-dillo meet a boy of about their own age who tells them that if they intend to support themselves by stealing they must seek the protection of Monipodio. It is clear from the outset that they are equally fascinated by what the boy tells them and the language he uses. Their conversation is a lesson in argot, *germanía*. Curiosity about the speech of the Seville underworld is surely one of the motives that lead them to seek out Monipodio, though of course it is not the only one.

When Rincón asks their new acquaintance whether he is a thief he answers that he is indeed, though not yet an ac-complished one:

—¿Es vuesa merced, por ventura, ladrón?
—Sí—respondió él—para servir a Dios y a las bue-nas gentes, aunque no de los muy cursados; que to-davía estoy en el año del noviciado.

A lo cual respondió Cortado:

—Cosa nueva es para mí que haya ladrones para servir a Dios y a la buena gente.

A lo cual respondió el mozo:

—Señor, yo no me meto en tologías; lo que sé es que cada uno en su oficio puede alabar a Dios, y más con la orden que tiene dada Monipodio a todos sus ahijados. [1:235]

⟨"Are you, Sir, a thief by any chance?"

"Indeed I am," the boy replied, "to serve God and decent people, though I'm not a skilled one, for I'm still serving my year as a novice."

"It's news to me," said Cortado, "that there are thieves who serve God and decent people."

To which the boy answered: "Sir, I don't medddle with thology; all I know is that everyone can praise God in his work, especially in view of the good order Monipodio imposes on all his godchildren."⟩

Cortadillo professes to be puzzled by the boy's use of the conventional courtesy formula "para servir a Dios y a la buena gente," to serve God and decent people. Cortadillo takes it literally and not just as another way of saying "at your service." The boy himself takes it equally literally, though he gives an odd interpretation to the phrase "servir a Dios." So do Monipodio and the other members of his gang.

The whole novella is a splendid illustration of Mikhail Bakhtin's view that "all languages of heteroglossia . . . are specific points of view on the world, forms for conceptualizing the world in words" (1981, 291-92). Bakhtin defines heteroglossia in literature as *"another's speech in another's language,* serving to express authorial intentions but in a refracted way. Such speech constitutes a special type of *double-voiced discourse.* It serves two speakers at the same time and expresses simultaneously two different intentions" (1981, 324). Heteroglossia is not just a literary device but a feature of the language of real life that may be exploited for literary purposes. The members of different social groups do not speak alike; professors do not speak like peasants nor soldiers like clergymen. For Bakhtin, "at any given moment of its historical existence, language is heteroglot from top to bottom" (ibid., 291) and all the languages that make up heteroglossia "encounter one another and coexist in the consciousness of real people" (ibid., 292).

Bakhtin's observation that "*Don Quixote*...realizes in itself, in extraordinary depth and breadth, all the artistic possibilities of heteroglot and internally dialogized novelistic discourse" (1981, 324) applies equally to *Rinconete y Cortadillo*. Monipodio and his followers have a language of their own, which awakens wonder (*admiratio*) in the two new recruits. Monipodio's organization is variously termed a guild or fraternity (*cofradía*, 1:239), a brotherhood (*hermandad*, 1:242), and a religious community (*congregación*, 1:240). The terms can hardly be translated into modern English, since they refer both to the religious life and to the seventeenth-century organization of workmen into a series of guilds that corresponded in some ways to modern trade unions; they differed from the latter in that their members included both masters and those who worked for them. It is clear that Monipodio and his henchmen think of their *cofradía* as a guild like other guilds, one that offers them protection against competition from outsiders and assumes responsibility for the religious obligations of its members, for example, by paying for the performance of masses for the dead. What surprises Rinconete and Cortadillo is not that a single organization should undertake functions that today would be divided among churches, trade unions, and social welfare agencies but that its members derive their income from crime, which they treat as a trade like any other. Monipodio is a precursor of Mr. Peachum, the receiver of stolen goods in John Gay's *Beggar's Opera* (1728); William Empson's brilliant analysis of Gay's play (1935) throws a great deal of light on Cervantes' novella.

The way in which Monipodio and his followers use language to disguise the way they earn their living is a form of role-playing. Like every kind of role-playing, it involves a measure of deception, as Castiglione's courtiers knew (Barish 1981, 170-72; Javitch 1983, 24). In *The Book of the Courtier* Signor Gaspar Pallavicino, the champion of old-fashioned honesty, objects to his companions' stress on the importance of *sprezzatura*, nonchalance, which he thinks dishonest because it attempts to conceal the effort that lies behind the courtier's accomplishments:

> Questa a me non par arte, ma vero inganno; né credo che si convenga, a chi vol esser omo da bene, mai lo ingannare. [2.40.252]
>
> ⟨This seems to me to be not an art, but an actual deceit; and I do not think it seemly for anyone who wishes to be a man of honor ever to deceive. [Singleton 1959, 138]⟩

Pallavicino's is of course a minority view. Most of the other participants in Castiglione's nostalgic evocation of the court of Urbino would agree with Messer Federico Fregoso that

> Questo ... è più presto un ornamento ... che inganno; e se pur è inganno, non è da biasimare. ... E se voi avete una gioia, la qual dislegata mostri esser bella, venendo poi alle mani d'un bon orefice, che col legarla bene la faccia parer molto più bella, non direte voi che quello orefice inganna gli occhi di chi la vede! [2.40.252-53]
>
> ⟨This ... is an ornament ... rather than deceit; and even if it be deceit, it is not to be censured. ... If you have a beautiful jewel with no setting, and it passes into the hands of a good goldsmith who with a skillful setting makes it appear far more beautiful, will you say that the goldsmith deceives the eye of the one who looks at it? [Singleton 1959, 138-39].⟩

Misuse of language entails a much greater risk than that of deceiving others: the risk of self-deception. Rinconete and

Cortadillo learn from Monipodio and his accomplices the danger of mistaking words for things, of being deceived by one's own use of language. What Rinconete rejects at the end of the novella is less the criminal life than the self-deception he sees in Monipodio and his henchmen. The speech in which Monipodio welcomes Rinconete and Cortadillo to his band of thieves and cutthroats is a superb example of what Bakhtin calls "double-voiced discourse":

—Pues de aquí adelante—respondió Monipodio—quiero y es mi voluntad que vos, Rincón, os llaméis *Rinconete*, y vos, Cortado, *Cortadillo*, que son nombres que asientan como de molde a vuestra edad y a nuestras ordenanzas, debajo de las cuales cae tener la necesidad de saber los nombres de los padres de nuestros cofrades, porque tenemos de costumbre de hacer decir cada año ciertas misas por las ánimas de nuestros difuntos y bienhechores, sacando el *estupendo* para la limosna de quien las dice de alguna parte de lo que *se garbea*, y estas tales misas, así dichas como pagadas, dicen que aprovechan a las tales ánimas por vía de *naufragio*; y caen debajo de nuestros bienhechores: el procurador que nos defiende, el *guro* que nos avisa, el verdugo que nos tiene lástima, el que cuando [alguno] de nosotros va huyendo por la calle y detrás le van dando voces: "¡Al ladrón, al ladrón! ¡Deténganle, deténganle!," uno se pone en medio y se opone al raudal de los que le siguen, diciendo: "¡Déjenle al cuitado, que harta malaventura lleva! ¡Allá se lo haya; castíguele su pecado!" Son también bienhechoras nuestras las *socorridas* que de su sudor nos socorren, así en la *trena* como en las *guras*; y también lo son nuestros padres y madres, que nos echan al mundo, y el escribano, que si anda de buena, no hay delito que lo sea ni culpa a quien se dé mucha pena; y por todos estos que he dicho hace nuestra hermandad cada año su *adversario* con la mayor *popa* y *soledad* que podemos. [1:241-42; my italics]

⟨"From now on," said Monipodio, "I desire and decree
that you, Rincón, be called 'Rinconete,' and you, Cortado, 'Cortadillo,' for these names are appropriate to
your age and to our statutes, which require us to know
the names of our fellow members, since it is our custom to have certain masses said every year for the
souls of our deceased members and for our benefactors,
paying the priest's *stupend* with part of our takings,
and these masses, duly said and paid for, are said to
benefit the said souls by way of *outrage*. Among our
benefactors are the lawyer who defends us, the police-
man who warns us, the executioner who takes pity on
us, the man who, when one of us is running away down
the street and someone yells after him "Stop thief! Stop
thief!" stands in the way and holds up the crowd that
follows him, saying "Let the poor devil go, he's already
had enough bad luck! It's his problem; let his sin be his
punishment!" Our benefactors also include the women
who use the money they've earned by the sweat of
their brow to help us when we are in prison or in the
galleys and our fathers and mothers, who bring us into
the world, and the clerk of court, who if he's on our
side can make sure that no one is found guilty of a
crime and that no guilt brings punishment; and every
year our brotherhood celebrates the *adversary* of all
those I've mentioned with the greatest *pop and solidity*
we can manage.⟩

The words and phrases I have italicized are partly terms
taken from the argot of the Seville underworld (*se garbea,
guro, socorridas, trena, guras*), partly malapropisms (*estupendo* for *estipendio, naufragio* for *sufragio, adversario* for
aniversario, popa y soledad for *pompa y solemnidad*). Both
consort oddly with the formality of Monipodio's discourse
in a splendid example of the play with different levels of language that Angel Rosenblat considers the most characteristic feature of Cervantes' style (1971, 205).

Monipodio is as fond of rhetorical figures as of high-
sounding words. His speech begins with an example of cir-

cumlocution or periphrasis (*quiero y es mi voluntad*) and continues with one of diaeresis, amplification by dividing genus (*nuestros bienhechores*) into species (*el guro, el verdugo*). It then dissolves into anacoluthon when he is unable to think of a name for his third type of benefactor, who enables a criminal to escape by distracting the crowd that pursues him. His second series of female benefactors, *nuestras bienhechoras*, collapses after a single example, *las socorridas*, and continues with examples that might more properly have been included in the first series. As we shall see, Monipodio's concern for the form rather than the substance of his speech, which he shares with the other members of his gang, will be a major factor in persuading the boys to leave his company of outlaws.

Rinconete's response (1:242) reveals his awareness of the two voices present in Monipodio's speech:

> Por cierto—dijo Rinconete, ya confirmado con este nombre—que es obra digna del altísimo y profundísimo ingenio que hemos oído decir que vuesa merced, señor Monipodio, tiene. Pero nuestros padres aun gozan de la vida; si en ella les alcanzáremos, daremos luego noticia a esta felicísima y abogada confraternidad, para que por sus almas se les haga ese *naufragio* o tormenta, o ese *adversario* que vuesa merced dice, con la solenidad y pompa acostumbrada, si ya no es que se hace mejor con *popa y soledad*, como también apuntó vuesa merced en sus razones. [1:242; my italics]

> ("Certainly," said Rinconete, now confirmed with this name, "it is a task worthy of the most lofty and profound talent, that, as we have heard, you, Señor Monipodio, possess. But our parents are still living; if we should hear of their deaths we shall immediately notify this most blessed and protective confraternity so that they may benefit from this outrage or tempest or that adversary you spoke of, with the customary pomp and solemnity, unless, of course, it would be better to do it with that pop and solidity to which you also alluded in your remarks.)

Rinconete uses none of the terms of criminal argot that had peppered Monipodio's speech. He repeats some of Monipodio's malapropisms (*naufragio, adversario, popa y soledad*) but quietly amends them, the rhetorical device of epanorthosis or *correctio*. His response demonstrates the truth of Bakhtin's assertion that "the ideological becoming of a human being . . . is the process of selectively assimilating the words of others" (1981, 341). Rinconete demonstrates that he can imitate Monipodio's way of speaking while keeping himself at a distance from the world view it implies.

Although Rinconete judges Monipodio's malapropisms as moral lapses, he makes no attempt to correct them. Castiglione's courtiers similarly recognize that they must sometimes hide their true feelings and even profess opinions they do not hold since their position depends on keeping the goodwill of their prince. This willingness to dissemble for the sake of expediency is quite lacking in Don Quixote, as it is lacking in Berganza in *El coloquio de los perros*, and helps to explain why both fail in their attempts to reform the corrupt world in which they find themselves, a point to which I shall return in chapter 6. Rinconete may be wiser, if less noble, in making no attempt to correct Monipodio's solecisms.

If Rinconete adopts some features of Monipodio's speech, so does the narrator. Cervantes' irony is often a kind of heteroglossia that reflects the way the characters perceive themselves, as in the simile of the frightened doves in the narrator's account of the criminals' behavior when a police officer visits Monipodio's headquarters:

Nunca ha disparado arcabuz a deshora, ni trueno repentino espantó así bandada de descuidadas palomas, como puso en alboroto y espanto a toda aquella recogida companía y buena gente la nueva de la venida del alcalde de la justicia. [1:263]

⟨Never did an unexpected shot from a harquebus nor a sudden burst of thunder frighten a band of carefree doves more than the news of the arrival of the Chief Magistrate terrified and disconcerted that happy company of good people.⟩

The same image of the frightened doves is used on two different occasions in *El celoso extremeño* (2:198, 2:210) with similar ironic effect.

There are other examples of heteroglossia on the part of the narrator: Monipodio is eagerly awaited by "the whole virtuous company" of his henchmen ("toda aquella virtuosa compañía," 1.239), which the narrator elsewhere calls a blessed community ("su compañía y bendita comunidad," 1:271). At the very end of the story he promises to tell of Rinconete's further adventures, which he refers to as "su vida y milagros" (1:272), his life and miracles, as if he were relating a saint's life.

Like Andrés and Preciosa in *La gitanilla* and Carriazo and Avendaño in *La ilustre fregona*, Rinconete sees clearly that he is playing a role. Though he engages in some petty crime and lives for a time among criminals, there is never any doubt that his moral standards are fundamentally the same as the reader's. There is no trace of irony in his condemnation of the morality of his new acquaintances, since he is always conscious of the distance that separates them from himself. Presumably he shares this sense of separateness with his younger companion.

Students of Cervantes' works have often noted his dislike of the picaresque novel. Rinconete and Cortadillo are not typical *pícaros*. They have not been rejected by their families and left to shift for themselves; there is no reference to the specter of hunger that haunts the pages of most picaresque narratives. Ruth El Saffar comments: "Not necessity, but the pleasure they derive from duping others motivates the series of tricks they play before being recruited for Monipodio's confraternity. . . . Whereas the pícaro may steal to get food, . . . in *Rinconete y Cortadillo*, . . . it is the dexterity, the ability to fool, that is elevated to central importance" (1974, 35).

Claudio Guillén's list of the major characteristics of the picaresque novel in his essay "Toward a Definition of the Picaresque" offers a handy measure of the distance that separates Cervantes' novella from a typical example of the genre (1971, 79-85). The most important is that "the *pícaro* is, first of all, an orphan. . . . He is obliged to fend for himself . . . in an environment *for which he is not prepared.* . . . All values must be rediscovered by him anew, as if by a godless Adam" (ibid., 79). Neither *Rinconete y Cortadillo* nor any of the other *Novelas ejemplares* sometimes considered picaresque—*La gitanilla, La ilustre fregona,* and *El coloquio de los perros*—offers protagonists who are obliged, like Guillén's typical pícaro, to *invent* a new set of values that will enable them to survive in a hostile environment.

The time Rinconete and Cortadillo spend with Monipodio's company is a variant of the sojourn in the pastoral oasis that we examined in connection with *La gitanilla.* A sense of holiday, of deliberately chosen release from the tedium of everyday life, pervades the whole novella. But if *Rinconete y Cortadillo* is suffused with the spirit of holiday, it is the kind of holiday from which one returns with a heightened sense of seriousness, a perfect example of the progression C. L. Barber thinks typical of one kind of pastoral and sums up in the phrase "through release to clarification" (1959, 6-10). To see the novella in these terms makes it difficult to agree with critics who argue that it ends inconclusively or with the moral downfall of the protagonists.

For Carlos Blanco Aguinaga, Monipodio's courtyard is "presented before two spectators who (like Cervantes and like the reader) make no judgment but rather, overawed, see and hear life in process. . . . No conclusion is reached and in this opening toward the future any moral commentary disappears. . . . The reader remains with the hope of more life, which is always possible" (1957, 338). Peter Dunn, too, holds that the ending is inconclusive (1973, 93). In a later study, however, Dunn takes a different view, seeing the boys' moral defeat as already assured: "Seeking picaresque freedom leads to the negation of freedom; *facilis descensus Averni.* . . .

Cervantes is representing a destiny implicit in an initial disposition. To choose the picaresque road is to choose Monipodio in the end. [Cervantes has managed] to disclose significance in a beginning, not an end; and while narrating not the past but the present of his boys, he has created for them a virtual future" (1982, 127-28).

The last paragraph of *Rinconete y Cortadillo* begins, however, with the narrator's assertion that Rinconete, despite his youth, was intelligent and of good character: "Era Rinconete, aunque muchacho, de muy buen entendimiento, y tenía un buen natural" (1:271). The narrator adds:

Sobre todo, le admiraba [a Rinconete] la seguridad que tenían [Monipodio y sus compañeros] y la confianza de irse al cielo con no faltar a sus devociones, estando tan llenos de hurtos, y de homicidios, y de ofensas de Dios. [1:272]

⟨Most of all, Rinconete was amazed that [Monipodio and his companions] were sure they would go to heaven, despite their many thefts, murders, and offenses against God, provided they did not fail to perform their devotions.⟩

The whole paragraph shows clearly that Rinconete has a code of values by which to judge Monipodio and his followers and that he sees them as quite different from himself. The narrator says explicitly that Rinconete will eventually reject Monipodio's world and that he will do so for reasons the reader may be expected to share. Rinconete does not postpone his departure because of any moral deficiency but solely because of his youth and inexperience:

Propuso en sí de aconsejar a su compañero no durasen mucho en aquella vida tan perdida y tan mala, tan inquieta, y tan libre y disoluta. Pero, con todo esto, llevado de sus pocos años y de su poca experiencia, pasó con ella adelante algunos meses. [1:272]

⟨He made up his mind to advise his companion that
they should not remain long in that life which was so
wretched and so evil, so hazardous, disorderly and dis-
solute. Nevertheless, carried away by his youth and inexperience, he remained for a few more months.⟩

This passage can hardly be taken as evidence of Cervantes'
moral neutrality. It seems designed rather to allay the reader's concern over what will become of Rinconete and Cortadillo by offering assurance that they will suffer no lasting
harm through their association with Monipodio.

Nineteenth-century realistic novels like Stendhal's *Le
Rouge et le noir* or Balzac's *Le Père Goriot* typically trace
the progress of the protagonist's corruption as a result of exposure to a corrupt world. *Rinconete y Cortadillo*, like *La
gitanilla*, *La ilustre fregona*, and *El amante liberal*, does just
the opposite. In all of them, the principal characters remain
unsullied by contact with a sordid reality. We shall see in
later chapters that the same is true of Leonora in *El celoso
extremeño* and of Berganza in *El coloquio de los perros*. Any
of them might serve as a refutation of Saint Paul's warning
that "evil communications corrupt good manners" (1 Cor.
15.33); bad companions may lead to bad consequences, but
they do not necessarily do so. Although both types of novel
may serve a didactic purpose, they teach different lessons.
The nineteenth-century novelists characteristically stress
the danger of taking the first step on the downward path and
the complicity of society in creating the conditions that lead
to the corruption of the protagonist. Cervantes, on the other
hand, stresses the individual's freedom to rise above his immediate circumstances and to remain true to a moral code
superior to that of the people around him. Like Don Juan de
Cárcamo or Berganza, Rinconete remains constantly aware
that he is playing a role he has deliberately chosen and that
he is free to reject whenever he wishes.

The ending of the novella should not be taken as tanta-
mount to saying that the boys will live happily ever after.
They will have other moral choices to make and there is no

guarantee that they will always choose wisely. But at least in this one case we have seen Rinconete make the right choice. His moral victory, however, does not insure that he will attain any sort of worldly success. Although moral success or failure is possible for anyone, worldly success in the *Novelas ejemplares* is reserved for those whose wealth or lineage places them in a favored position.

Like Don Juan de Cárcamo in *La gitanilla* or Ricardo in *El amante liberal*, Rinconete exemplifies the flexibility Castiglione's courtiers valued so highly. Like some other sixteenth-century writers, Castiglione had an almost unlimited faith in man's ability to fashion himself into something more nearly approaching his own ideal. By the end of the century this faith was beginning to come under increasingly heavy attack. Both the Protestant reformers and their Catholic adversaries now stressed rather man's inability to transform himself by his own efforts. Thomas Greene has traced the rise and fall of the Renaissance conception of the flexibility of the self in a fine essay, in which he asserts that "Renaissance speculation on the theme of flexibility reaches a natural end-point with the plays of Shakespeare. . . . One of the first comedies, *Love's Labor's Lost*, makes game of men who are maladroit at shifting roles and disguises, and in most of the rest the palm goes to the quicksilver wit, the alert, the volatile, the adroit improviser. . . . The tragedies, on the other hand, dramatize typically a stubborn rigidity, heroically or blindly tardy in its adaptations, dooming the protagonist to an agonizing and belated evolution upward toward tragic wisdom" (1968, 262-63). Greene contrasts Shakespeare's treatment of the flexibility of the self with that of Cervantes in *Don Quixote:*

It is very unlikely that Shakespeare was conscious of rejecting an age. It is much more likely that Cervante was so conscious. Whatever his awareness, Cervantes wrote the most powerful of all attacks upon the transforming imagination, most powerful probably because most sympathetic. The knight of La Mancha is so lovable a caricature because his rigidity is so pure, and his will for a world made new so movingly inflexible. But he is already *old* in 1605: he belongs to a past that is suddenly seen to be decayed. With the intuitive recognition across the continent that Don Quixote's hope was tragically anachronistic, an age was over. Europe was left with the resignation of the earthbound, and with the novel, which teaches through disillusionment. [ibid., 263-64]

Some of the *Novelas ejemplares* offer a more hopeful view of the flexibility of the self than does *Don Quixote*. One of the attractions of pastoral for Cervantes, as for some of his contemporaries, including of course Shakespeare, must have been that it gave him an opportunity to let his characters experiment with unfamiliar roles and demonstrate their ability to play them skillfully while remaining true to a code of values quite different from that of a person born to the social role they have chosen. Neither Don Juan de Cárcamo nor Preciosa really behaves like a gypsy, any more than Don Diego de Carriazo in *La ilustre fregona* behaves like a pícaro or his companion Don Tomás de Avendaño like a *mozo de mesón*. Rinconete and Cortadillo, though certainly of humbler origin than any of these, similarly remain true to a moral code that keeps them from identifying completely with the members of Monipodio's brotherhood of thieves.

In his essay "The Noble Rider and the Sound of Words," Wallace Stevens writes of the Renaissance conception of nobility as a subject for poetry no longer available in our time: "poetry," he asserts, "is a cemetery of nobilities" (1965, 35). As an example of the kind of nobility he has in mind, Stevens adduces Verrocchio's equestrian statue of Bartolomeo Colleoni in Venice:

There, on the edge of the world in which we live today, [Verrocchio] established a form of such nobility that it has never ceased to magnify us in our own eyes. It is like the form of an invincible man, who has come, slowly and boldly, through every warlike opposition of the past and who moves in our midst without dropping the bridle of the powerful horse from his hand, without taking off his helmet and without relaxing the attitude of a warrior of noble origin. What man on whose side the horseman fought could ever be anything but fearless, anything but indomitable? One feels the passion of rhetoric begin to stir and even to grow furious; and one thinks that, after all, the noble style, in whatever it creates, merely perpetuates the noble style. In this statue, the apposition between reality and the imagination is too favorable to the imagination. [ibid., 8]

The statue "seems, nowadays, what it may very well not have seemed a few years ago, a little overpowering, a little magnificent" (ibid., 9). Stevens adds: "Undoubtedly, Don Quixote could be Bartolomeo Colleoni in Spain. . . . The difference between them is that Verrocchio believed in one kind of nobility and Cervantes, if he believed in any, believed in another kind. With Verrocchio it was an affair of the noble style, whatever his prepossession respecting the nobility of man as a real animal may have been. With Cervantes, nobility was not a thing of the imagination. It was a part of reality, it was something that exists in life, something so true to us that it is in danger of ceasing to exist, if we isolate it, something in the mind of a precarious tenure" (ibid., 9). Stevens' view of Don Quixote as a noble figure is the romantic one held by many modern readers. There are good reasons for doubting that it was held by Cervantes' first readers and even perhaps by Cervantes himself (Russell 1969; see also Close 1978). Stevens' view is more applicable to some of the *Novelas ejemplares*.

For many readers, some of the *Novelas ejemplares* are works in which "the apposition between reality and the imagination is too favorable to the imagination." Jennifer Lowe, for example, says that Preciosa in *La gitanilla* "is somewhat over-sentimentalised for our taste, . . . too sweet, far too pink and white, literally and metaphorically" (1971, 52). But the world of the gypsies in which Preciosa moves, although certainly not depicted realistically, has not been ennobled to make it more worthy of her. It is as if Verrocchio had seated Colleoni not on a magnificent charger but on a broken-down nag—a Rocinante—in order to suggest that anyone whose nobility can shine forth in such circumstances must be noble indeed.

Exactly the same thing may be said of Cervantes' noblemen turned pícaros Don Juan de Cárcamo in *La gitanilla* and Carriazo and Avendaño in *La ilustre fregona* as well as of his heroine Costanza in the latter novella. It is perhaps equally, though less obviously, true of Rinconete and Cortadillo. For all of them their sojourn in a picaresque counterpart of the pastoral oasis allows their innate good qualities to shine forth all the more brightly. Their stay among their moral inferiors gives them an opportunity to reveal what they essentially are: persons whose nobility does not depend on their circumstances. It is not "an affair of the noble style," as Stevens says of Verrocchio's statue of Colleoni, but "a part of reality, . . . something that exists in life."

CHAPTER 5

Frustrated Expectations:
El celoso extremeño

In 1788, while cataloging the library of San Isidro in Madrid, Isidoro Bosarte discovered a manuscript, now lost, that contained versions of *Rinconete y Cortadillo* and *El celoso extremeño* different from those published in the *Novelas ejemplares* in 1613. Most of the differences between the two versions of the two novellas are stylistic, but one of those in *El celoso extremeño* is a striking exception: in the manuscript the young wife Isabela, as Leonora is called in this version, allows herself to be seduced by Loaysa, while in the printed version she successfully defends herself against his attempts to make love to her.

Most readers of the *Novelas ejemplares* would surely agree with A. F. Lambert that the new ending "transform[s] the *dénouement* and, retroactively, the entire story" (1980, 219). Lambert notes also that in the final version "Cervantes omits or tones down burlesque elements from the Porras version" (ibid., 229). He left many others unchanged. The new ending found in the printed version does not alter the fact that much of the action that precedes it is funny.

The theme of the old man who marries a young wife appears again in Cervantes' one-act farce *El viejo celoso*, published only a few months before his death in April 1616. The farce may have served as a preliminary sketch for the novella, though Eugenio Asensio believes that the novella was written first (Cervantes 1970, 25). In the play the wife concedes that her husband provides her generously with clothes and jewels but complains bitterly that he keeps her a prisoner in her own house:

Que no quiero riquezas, señora Ortigosa; que me so-
bran las joyas, y me ponen en confusión las diferencias
de colores de mis muchos vestidos; . . . más vestida me
tiene que un palmito, y con más joyas que la vedriera
de un platero rico. No me clavara él las ventanas, cer-
rara las puertas, visitara a todas horas la casa, dester-
rara della los gatos y los perros, solamente porque
tienen nombre de varón; que, a trueco de que no
hiciera esto y otras cosas no vistas en materia de recato
yo le perdonara sus dádivas y mercedes. . . . Le vendían
el otro día una tapicería a bonísimo precio, y por ser de
figuras no la quiso, y compró otra de verduras, por
mayor precio, aunque no era tan buena. Siete puertas
hay antes que se llegue a mi aposento, fuera de la puer-
ta de la calle, y todas se cierran con llave, y las llaves
no me ha sido posible averiguar dónde las esconde de
noche. [Cervantes 1970, 205-06]

⟨I don't want to be rich, Señora Hortigosa; I have more
jewels than I know what to do with and so many
dresses of different colors that I can't begin to keep
track of them. . . . [Cañizares] keeps me dressed to the
nines and with more jewels than you'd find in a rich
silversmith's showcase. If only he wouldn't nail up the
windows, lock the doors, watch the house all the time,
and drive away tomcats and dogs just because people
call them by men's names, if he would give up these
and other unheard-of precautions I'd be glad to do
without favors and gifts. . . . The other day he had a
chance to buy a tapestry at a very good price and he refused because it had human figures on it; instead he
bought another decorated with leaves that wasn't as
good and cost more to boot. You have to pass through
seven locked doors to get to my room, not counting the
one that opens onto the street, and I've never been able
to discover where he keeps the keys at night.⟩

Cervantes surely expected his readers to laugh at this and it
is hard to believe that they did not laugh when they met the

same motifs in *El celoso extremeño*. Carrizales, like his counterpart Cañizares in the interlude,

> no consintió que dentro de su casa hubiese algún animal que fuese varón. A los ratones de ella jamás los persiguió gato, ni en ella se oyó ladrido de perro; todas eran del género femenino. . . . Jamás entró hombre de la puerta adentro del patio. . . . Las figuras de los paños que sus salas y cuadras adornaban, todas eran hembras, flores y boscajes. [2:184]

> ⟨refused to have any male animal in his house. No tomcat ever chased his rats nor did any male dog ever bark there; only females were allowed to enter. . . . No man ever passed the door of the inner court . . . The figures in the tapestries that adorned his walls were all of women, flowers, and woodland scenes.⟩

Both Carrizales and Cañizares exemplify the proverb cited by the seventeenth-century collector Gonzalo de Correas: "Marido zeloso, nunka tiene rreposo," a jealous husband knows no rest (1967, 526).

No single source has been discovered for *El celoso extremeño*. Cervantes' contemporaries must have considered it a reworking of familiar materials whose potential for comedy had been explored by many other writers as well as in the oral tales that formed an important part of the entertainment of all classes and not just of those who had no access to books (Chevalier 1975, 1978). The novella combines several well-known folktale motifs. The most important are that of the husband who imprisons his wife in a house or tower in order to preserve her chastity, motif T381.0.2 in Stith Thompson's classification, and foolish old man marries young girl, motif J445.2. A minor motif is K1349.4, young man gains access to a woman's room by charming her guard with music.

The narrator presents Carrizales' unreasoning jealousy without explanation, as if he were a character in a folktale: "de su natural condición era el más celoso hombre del mundo" (2:179). In Cervantes' title *celoso* is the noun and *extremeño* the adjective, rather than the other way round, as in the usual English translation *The Jealous Extremaduran*. Carrizales is a member of the class of men whose dominant trait is jealousy. He is also, not quite incidentally, from Extremadura, whose inhabitants were believed to be unusually prone to jealousy (Molho 1990, 746). In the title of the interlude *El viejo celoso,* on the other hand, *celoso* is an adjective, preceded by the noun *viejo*. In the play Cañizares is not a jealous man who is old but an old man who is jealous, a point underscored by his servant when she says that he is "viejo y reviejo y más que viejo" and that she never tires of repeating that he is old, "no me puedo hartar de decille viejo" (Cervantes 1970, 206).

A further link with popular tradition is provided by the *villancico* sung by the duenna Marialonso (2:208-209), which begins

> Madre, la mi madre,
> guardas me ponéis,
> *que si yo no me guardo,*
> *no me guardaréis.* [2:208]

⟨Mother, you have guards to watch me, but if I don't guard myself, no one else can guard me.⟩

The song is found in several contemporary collections and survives today in the oral traditions of several Spanish provinces; Cervantes uses it again in his play *La entretenida* (Torner 1966, 198-201). It is a lyric elaboration of a well-known proverb; Correas cites it in three different forms: "A la ke kiere ser mala, poko aprovecha guardarla; o por demás es guardarla; o por demás será guardarla" (1967, 6).

The song underscores Carrizales' foolishness in refusing to heed conventional wisdom. It is ideally suited to Marialonso's purposes: to arouse Leonora's desire for Loaysa and to persuade her that she can free herself from her husband's control if only she will make up her mind to do so—and also, of course, to give Marialonso an opportunity to satisfy her own desire for him. The first stanza describes both the state of mind she hopes to foster in her mistress and her own frustration at being forced to share Leonora's confinement:

> Dicen que está escrito,
> y con gran razón,
> ser la privación
> causa de apetito;
> crece en infinito
> encerrado amor;
> por eso es mejor
> que no me encerréis;
> *que si yo no me guardo*
> *no me guardaréis.* [2:208]

⟨They say it is written, and justly so, that lack stimulates appetite; love increases when the lover is confined; therefore it is useless to confine me, for if I do not guard myself, you cannot guard me.⟩

Like many other elements in the novella, the song must have made Cervantes' contemporaries feel that they were reading a conventional funny story that would end with the triumph of the young lovers, like the interlude *El viejo celoso*. But the expectations aroused by the song prove false: when the crucial moment arrives, Leonora successfully defends her virtue.

Like the proverbial expressions that inspired it, the song does not say that a woman has no need of *guardas* to protect her; it says only that *guardas* alone are not enough. In his popular manual of advice to women, *La perfecta casada* (*The Perfect Wife*), first published in 1583, Fray Luis de León asserts emphatically that a woman's place is in the home:

> ¿Por qué les dió a las mujeres Dios las fuerzas flacas y los miembros, sino porque las crió . . . para estar en su rincón asentadas? Su natural propio perverte la mujer callejera. Y como los peces, en cuanto están dentro del agua, discurren por ella y andan y vuelan ligeros, mas,

si acaso los sacan de allí, quedan sin se poder menear,
así la buena mujer, cuanto para de sus puertas adentro
ha de ser presta y ligera, tanto para fuera de ellas se ha
de tener por coja y torpe. Y pues no las dotó Dios ni del
ingenio que piden los negocios mayores, ni de las fuer-
zas que son menester para la guerra y el campo, mí-
danse con lo que son y conténtense con lo que es de su
suerte, y entiendan en su casa y anden en ella, pues las
hizo Dios para ella sola. Los chinos, en naciendo, les
tuercen a las niñas los pies, porque, cuando sean mujeres, no los tengan para salir fuera, y porque, para an-
dar en su casa, aquellos torcidos les bastan. [1951, 324]

⟨Why did God make women weak if not so that they
might remain seated in their corners? The woman who
spends her time outside in the street perverts her true
nature. And as fish, which move rapidly and freely in
water, cannot move when they are taken out of it, so
the virtuous woman must be active at home while
outside it she appears lame and clumsy. And since God
has not granted women either the intelligence needed
for important enterprises or the strength needed for
war or work in the fields, they should consider what
they are and content themselves with the activities
suited to them, and look to the management of their
houses and keep busy in them, since God made them
for this alone. The Chinese twist girls' feet when they
are born so that when they grow up they will be unable
to leave their houses where those deformed feet are all
they need.⟩

The norm Fray Luis recommends is brutally summed up in
another maxim cited by Correas: "La muxer kasada i hon-
rada, la pierna kebrada y en kasa", an honest wife should
stay home with a broken leg (1967, 206). The proverb is still
current in Spain and expresses a widespread folk belief about
the proper behavior of women, as Pitt-Rivers notes with special reference to Andalusia (1966, 45).

Fray Luis's views are so shocking to modern readers that it must be emphasized that they are not at all exceptional, as Ian Maclean's survey of Renaissance views of women makes clear. While it is unlikely that Cervantes himself accepted them at face value (Wilson 1991), most of his contemporaries certainly did. For many Renaissance thinkers, woman's "assumed frailty of body, which best befits her for the care of the young and makes her unsuited to exposure to the dangers of the outside world, is accompanied by mental and emotional weaknesses which are the natural justification for her exclusion from public life, responsibility, and moral fulfilment" (Maclean 1980, 43-44). As a result, "in marriage, the rôles (*officia*) of man and wife are different, and this is often ascribed to the differing physical and mental attributes of the sexes. Man, more robust and audacious, is better suited for a peripatetic, outdoor, public, acquisitive rôle; woman, more timid, possessing judgement and physical force in lesser measure, is naturally the custodian of children, household goods, and the acquisitions of her husband ([Aristotle,] *Economics*, 1.3 [1343*b* 27ff]). . . . Woman's private existence in the home also prevents her from exciting concupiscence by public appearances: religious moralists are emphatic on this point" (ibid., 57-58). Many of Cervantes' seventeenth-century readers no doubt agreed with Fray Luis de León that "como son los hombres para lo público, así las mujeres para el encerramiento; y como es de los hombres el hablar y el salir a luz, así de ellas el encerrarse y encubrirse" (1951, 324). Maurice Molho (1990, 752) cites several Spanish proverbs that suggest that a woman who allows herself to appear at a window, and thus to be seen by persons who are not members of her household, is no better than a prostitute: "moza que asoma a la ventana a cada rato, quiérese vender barato." At the very least she is unlikely to prove a faithful wife: "joven ventanera, mala mujer casera."

Leonora is not the only Cervantine heroine shielded from contact with everyone except the members of her immediate family and its female servants. In *La fuerza de la sangre*,

Leocadia assures the man who has raped her that he need not fear she will recognize his voice, since she has never spoken to any man other than her father and her confessor (2:152); she is sixteen, a year older than Leonora. Dorotea, in *Don Quixote*, similarly says that she has spent her life

> en tantas ocupaciones y en un encerramiento tal, que al de un monesterio pudiera compararse, sin ser vista, a mi parecer, de otra persona alguna que de los criados de casa, porque los días que iba a misa era tan de mañana, y tan acompañada de mi madre y de otras criadas, y yo tan cubierta y tan recatada que apenas vían mis ojos más tierra de aquella donde ponía los pies. [1.28.349]

> ⟨busily and in a solitude like that of a convent, and so far as I knew without being seen by anyone except the servants, because on the days I attended mass I went so early, so closely attended by my mother and the other women of our household and so thickly veiled and so shy that my eyes scarcely saw anything but the ground I walked on.⟩

A most important difference separates Leonora from Leocadia and Dorotea: the latter are unmarried. The real oddity in Carrizales' treatment of Leonora is that he deals with her like a daughter rather than a wife. Melveena McKendrick notes: "Daughters were closely supervised; unmarried they were a liability, marriageable they were a valuable commodity, and if the sale was to be satisfactory the goods had to be kept in pristine condition. But wives . . . were a different matter: mistresses of their own houses, they enjoyed a freedom they denied their daughters" (1984, 331). Carrizales treats Leonora like a child, pampering her with dolls and candy rather than entrusting her with the care of the household, although conventional wisdom held that wives must be kept busy for their own protection. Fray Luis de León devotes an entire chapter of *La perfecta casada* to the proposition that women should have plenty to do, since they are naturally inclined to idleness and hence to sin: "cuanto de suyo es la mujer más inclinada al regalo y más fácil a en-

mollecerse y desatarse con el ocio, tanto el trabajo le con-
viene más" (1951, 278). In treating Leonora as a daughter
rather than as a wife, Carrizales reveals his fear that she will
betray him and in doing so lays the groundwork for his own
undoing, since the measures he takes to ensure that she has
no opportunity to be unfaithful tempt Loaysa to try to seduce her.

Most readers would probably say that *El celoso extremeño* begins as comedy and ends as tragedy. Northrop Frye
has pointed out that comedy

> has been remarkably tenacious of its structural princi-
> ples and character types. Bernard Shaw remarked that
> a comic dramatist could get a reputation for daring
> originality by stealing his method from Molière and
> his characters from Dickens: if we were to read
> Menander and Aristophanes for Molière and Dickens,
> the statement would be hardly less true. . . .
>
> The plot structure of Greek new comedy, as trans-
> mitted by Plautus and Terence, in itself less a form
> than a formula, has become the basis for most com-
> edy. . . . What normally happens is that a young man
> wants a young woman, that his desire is resisted by
> some opposition, usually paternal, and that near the
> end of the play some twist in the plot enables the hero
> to have his will. . . . [T]he movement of comedy is usu-
> ally a movement from one kind of society to another.
> At the beginning of the play the obstructing characters
> are in charge of the play's society, and the audience rec-
> ognizes that they are usurpers. At the end of the play
> the device in the plot that brings hero and heroine to-
> gether causes a new society to crystallize around the
> hero, and the moment when this crystallization occurs
> is the point of resolution in the action, the comic dis-
> covery, *anagnorisis* or *cognitio*. [1957, 163]

Frye's discussion throws a great deal of light on both the
structure and the characters of *El celoso extremeño*.

Alban Forcione's observation that *El celoso extremeño* "is about a man who is fanatically convinced of the value of objects and views people as objects" (1982, 36) applies equally to Carrizales and to Loaysa. The novella centers on two rival monomaniacs who are frustrated in their plans to outwit each other. The reader, who has been led to anticipate a comic resolution, is similarly frustrated in his expectations. Carrizales' role is that of the *senex iratus,* or heavy father, but with the important difference that he is not Leonora's father but her husband. In a society where divorce is unknown this means that the conventional comic resolution is possible only after his death. The new society that crystallizes around Leonora at the end of the story—the world of the convent—excludes not only Carrizales and Loaysa but all the other characters in the story, quite contrary to the comic norm, which, as Frye says, tends "to include as many people as possible in its final society: the blocking characters are more often reconciled or converted than simply repudiated" (1957, 165).

Loaysa's role is similarly traditional. In Frye's terms he is an *eiron* figure, the young hero, a role here combined with that of the tricky slave (*dolosus servus*) of Roman comedy, who hatches the schemes that enable the young man to get the girl. The female counterpart of the tricky slave is the *dueña* Marialonso, who is instrumental in persuading her mistress to allow Loaysa to enter the house. The black slave Luis and the two *negras bozales,* African slave girls who speak imperfect Spanish, are also established comic types; Frye notes that Renaissance comedy, unlike Roman comedy, introduced a large number of buffoon types, some of them with distinctive forms of speech like malapropisms or foreign accents (1957, 175).

As in Roman comedy, Leonora is reduced for the greater part of the novella almost to the level of a *muta persona.* She is what Elder Olson calls a situational character, deliberately kept in the background in order to keep the reader from feeling too much sympathy for her and thus preventing the elimination of the ground of concern that Olson considers an essential attribute of comedy (1968, 57-58, 78-79). Until almost the end of the novella Leonora is hardly more than an object; her role is comparable to that of the chest of money that obsesses Molière's Harpagon (cf. Molho 1990, 749).

When does the turn from comedy to tragedy take place? From the beginning there are hints that the novella will not turn out to be just another story about the cuckolding of a foolish old husband by an astute young wife. The action is displaced from the indeterminate setting of folktale to seventeenth-century Seville. Both Carrizales and Loaysa are identified as members of well-defined social groups. Carrizales is an *indiano rico,* a man who has returned to Spain after making his fortune in the New World, a type especially associated with Extremadura. His decision to settle in Seville rather than return to his native village is exceptional (Altman 1989, 3) and is presented by Cervantes as due to his desire to avoid being asked for money by his impoverished countrymen (2:178-79).

Loaysa, too, belongs to a familiar social type:

Hay en Sevilla un género de gente ociosa y holgazana . . . gente baldía, atildada y meliflua, de la cual y de su traje y manera de vivir, de su condición y de las leyes que guardan entre sí, había mucho que decir; pero por buenos respetos se deja. [2:184-85]

⟨There is in Seville a class of idle people who are good for nothing . . . worthless, presumptuous, well-spoken, about whom, and their dress and way of life, their social position and the rules they observe among themselves, there would be a lot to say; but for the sake of decency we shall say nothing.⟩

Loaysa is not in love with Leonora; he decides to seduce her even before he has seen her:

Asestó a mirar la casa del recatado Carrizales, y viéndola siempre cerrada, le tomó gana de saber quién vivía

dentro. . . . Supo la condición del viejo, de la hermo-
sura de su esposa y el modo que tenía en guardarla;
todo lo cual le encendió el deseo de ver si sería posible
expugnar, por fuerza o por industria, fortaleza tan
guardada. [2:185]

⟨He chanced to notice the house of the cautious Carrizales, and, seeing it always closed, was seized with a
desire to know who lived in it. . . . He learned of the
old man's jealousy, his wife's beauty, and the watch he
kept over her; all of which aroused his desire to see
whether he could succeed, through force or cunning, in
storming such a fortress.⟩

He is attracted precisely by the difficulty of gaining access to
Leonora as his insistence on informing his friends of his
plan and its progress makes clear. His primary goal is to win
their admiration for his cleverness and boldness. Loaysa is
very different from the young lovers, almost interchangeable from one play to the next, who compete with elderly
rivals in Roman comedy and in such lineal descendants as
Molière's L'Avare and L'Ecole des femmes. The demonic
qualities Cervantes associates with him have been well analyzed by Forcione (1982, 48-50). I find it hard to agree with
Lambert that "most readers surely enjoyed and will enjoy
Loaysa's efforts to seduce Leonora and cuckold Carrizales,
and innocently desire the young man success in his efforts
to penetrate the grotesque convent-prison erected by the old
man" (1980, 226).

Leonora, too, is very different from the malcasada, the
unhappy wife, who is a familiar figure in Spanish folk songs
and their courtly analogues (Romeu Figueras 1965, 1:97 and
2:362-64; Torner 1966, 282-85). The narrator stresses that
she is still a child who spends her days playing with dolls
and preparing sweets in the kitchen with her servants
(2:182). Unlike her counterpart Lorenza in El viejo celoso,
Leonora is not dissatisfied with her husband's performance
as a lover; the narrator says explicitly that Carrizales

comenzó a gozar como pudo los frutos del matrimonio, los cuales a Leonora, como no tenía experiencia de otros, ni eran gustosos ni desabridos. [2:182]

⟨began to enjoy so far as he could the pleasures of matrimony, which Leonora, since she had no experience of others, found neither pleasant nor unpleasant.⟩

Leonora is not greatly troubled by her confinement:

Su demasiada guarda le parecía advertido recato; pensaba y creía que lo que ella pasaba pasaban todas las recién casadas. No se desmandaban sus pensamientos a salir de las paredes de su casa, ni su voluntad deseaba otra cosa más de aquella que la de su marido quería. [2:184]

⟨Her husband's excessive vigilance seemed to her sensible caution; she thought and believed that all new wives were treated in the same way. Her thoughts never strayed beyond the walls of her house nor did she desire anything other than to keep her husband contented.⟩

The reader may easily overlook the one hint of Leonora's future conduct since it is presented as further evidence of her youth and inexperience:

La plata de las canas del viejo a los ojos de Leonora parecían cabellos de oro puro, porque el amor primero que las doncellas tienen se les imprime en el alma como el sello en la cera. [2:184]

⟨In Leonora's eyes the old man's gray hair was pure gold, since a maiden's first love leaves an imprint on her soul as a seal does on wax.⟩

If Carrizales had succeeded in making it impossible for Leonora to deceive him, he would have made it equally impossible for her to be truly virtuous. Fray Luis de Granada, whose *Libro de la oración* and *Guía de pecadores* were

among the books most frequently reprinted in the Golden
Age (Whinnom 1980, 194), asserts:

> Es perfecta virtud la que tentada no cae, que provocada
> no es vencida. . . . Así no es perfectamente honrada
> la mujer que guarda su honestidad sin haberla nadie
> provocado, sino la que tentada de muchas maneras,
> conserva entero y sin mancilla el pudor. [quoted in
> Forcione 1982, 77n]

> ⟨Perfect virtue does not fall when tempted and is not
> defeated when put to the test. . . . Thus a woman
> whose virtue has not been tested is not perfectly vir-
> tuous, but rather one who, though tested in many
> ways, keeps her honor intact and unsullied.⟩

The point Fray Luis makes is made more pithily in a proverb
cited by Correas: "Akélla es onrrada fina ke lo es konbatida;
i si es onrrada sin konbate, no se ensalze" (1967, 69). There
can be no doubt that Cervantes was familiar with this kind
of reasoning. A grotesque perversion of it serves as the basis
for Anselmo's plan to test the fidelity of his wife Camila in
El curioso impertinente (Neuschäfer 1990, 612-13). Anselmo
tells his friend Lotario that

> yo tengo para mí . . . que no es una mujer más buena de
> cuanto es o no es solicitada, y que aquella sola es fuerte
> que no se dobla a las promesas, a las dádivas, a las lágri-
> mas y a las continuas importunidades de los solícitos
> amantes. . . . Ansí que la que es buena por temor, o por
> falta de lugar, yo no la quiero tener en aquella estima
> en que tendré a la solicitada y perseguida, que salió con
> la corona del vencimiento. [1.33.403]

> ⟨for my part, I believe that a woman's virtue is no
> greater than the extent to which it has or has not been
> tested and that the only really strong woman is one
> who does not give in to the promises, gifts, tears and
> persistent entreaties of attentive suitors . . . Thus I do

not hold a woman who is virtuous through fear or lack
of opportunity in the same esteem as I do one who has
been tempted and tested and has emerged with the
crown of victory.⟩

Carrizales, of course, does not seek to test Leonora as
Anselmo tests Camila. On the contrary, he keeps her a prisoner because he feels sure she will be unable to resist temptation if she is allowed to confront it. In fact, of course,
Leonora does not yield to temptation, but that she does not
has nothing to do with the elaborate precautions her husband takes to shield her. It rests solely on her insistence on
taking full responsibility for her actions, a responsibility
Carrizales tries in vain to deny her.

El celoso extremeño has sometimes been seen as an example of Baroque *desengaño*, a term often translated as
"disillusion." Desengaño, however, does not suggest disap-
pointment but rather something positive, a stripping away
of illusion, an awakening to reality. Whether Carrizales experiences anything of this kind is questionable. He may simply be disappointed at the failure of his attempt to make it
impossible for Leonora to deceive him. Stephen Lipmann argues that "Carrizales remains *zeloso*, the victim of fears
that prevent him from seeing Leonora as she is and understanding how she used her free will to preserve the sanctity
of their marriage" (1986, 119; see also Williamson 1990, 807).

Edwin Williamson has warned against exaggerating Leonora's virtue, noting that Cervantes "seems to want to in-
dicate a certain degree of culpability when he writes
'Llegóse en esto el día, y cogió a los nuevos adúlteros enlaza-
dos en la red de sus brazos' [at this moment dawn broke and
revealed the new adulterers entwined in each other's arms]"
(1990, 806). Leonora is nevertheless justified in telling Carrizales that she has offended him only in intention: "sabed
que no os he ofendido sino con el pensamiento" (2:220). As
A. F. Lambert notes, "There is a vital distinction between
being tempted to sin and having the intention to sin. Leonora is gravely tempted, but finally resists" (1980, 226). She

makes no further attempt to convince her husband of her innocence, and we are given no hint as to her reasons for not
doing so, a point to which the narrator calls attention:

> Sólo no sé qué fue la causa que Leonora no puso más
> ahinco en disculparse y dar a entender a su celoso
> marido cuán limpia y sin ofensa había quedado en
> aquel suceso. [2:221]

> ⟨The one thing I do not know is why Leonora did not
> try harder to justify her conduct and to make her jeal-
> ous husband understand how pure and innocent she
> had remained on that occasion.⟩

The narrator says nothing about Leonora's reasons for making no real attempt to convince her husband of her innocence nor about why she changes her mind and decides not
to surrender to Loaysa after the duenna has persuaded her to
see him. His failure to explain Leonora's motives is one reason for the dissatisfaction felt by readers who find the conclusion of the story lacking in verisimilitude.

The conventions available to Cervantes gave writers little opportunity to examine a character's inner thoughts. As
Dorrit Cohn observes, "avoidance of psycho-narration . . .
dominates the third-person novel well into the nineteenth
century. While prolonged inside views were largely re-
stricted to first-person forms, third-person novels dwelt on
manifest behavior, with the characters' inner selves revealed
only indirectly through spoken language and telling ges-
ture" (1978, 21). Renaissance writers had, of course, other
ways of examining the inner lives of their characters. One is
the use of monologue. Robert Scholes and Robert Kellogg
note that "monologues tend to be rhetorical in what we call
romance and psychological in what we call realistic narrative. This distinction is, in fact, as crucial and as basic as
any which can be made to distinguish the two forms" (1966,
188). This is true of Cervantes' practice in the *Novelas
ejemplares*, where long, rhetorically complex speeches are
found primarily in the novellas that today are often consid-

ered romances. True monologues are nevertheless very rare in the *Novelas ejemplares;* the only example in the novellas considered in this book is Ricardo's apostrophe to the ruins of Nicosia at the beginning of *El amante liberal.* Most of the long discourses that many modern readers find unconvincing are not monologues but speeches addressed to another character and intended to influence his or her behavior. Because of this element of persuasion, and therefore of deliberate intention on the part of the speaker, they cannot be considered examples of what Cohn calls psycho-narration.

Neither can the wonderful conversations between Don Quixote and Sancho Panza in Cervantes' great novel. Their conversations are almost always primarily rhetorical in the sense that the knight and his squire try to persuade each other to act in a particular way or to change his mind about some disputed point. If the conversations are frequently also psychologically revealing, it is because the line of argument chosen by the speaker makes clear his understanding, sometimes incomplete or mistaken, of the mental processes of his interlocutor, or because they disclose something about himself that he wishes to conceal or fails to perceive.

Cervantes rarely uses either monologue or dialogue to enter the minds of Carrizales and Leonora. Real dialogue between them is impossible, for Leonora is too young and inexperienced to understand her husband's fears, while he is too self-centered to be interested in finding out what she thinks. After Carrizales' brief initial statement of his reasons for choosing Leonora as his wife, presented as an unspoken soliloquy (*hablando consigo mismo,* 2:179), he does not speak again until near the end of the novella (2:215); his one long speech, addressed not to Leonora but to her parents (2:217-19), is delivered as he lies dying. We never hear him speak directly to his wife, in marked contrast to Arnolphe in Molière's *L'Ecole des femmes,* who is onstage almost throughout the play and speaks more than half its lines. Carrizales makes no attempt to teach Leonora her duties as a wife. He concentrates all his energies on making it impossible for her to be unfaithful to him; nothing in Cervantes'

novella corresponds to the scene in which Molière's Arnolphe makes Agnès read the Maxims of Marriage. Carrizales
lacks the arrogance and complacence evident in Arnolphe's
ridicule of other husbands whose wives have deceived them,
as Leonora lacks the combination of innocence and sexual
excitement that characterizes Agnès. It is because we are
told so little about the inner lives of Carrizales and Leonora
that the developments at the end of the novella are so surprising. They excite admiratio because they go counter to all
our expectations.

Leonora should not be seen as the tragic victim of a re-
pressive society that allowed a woman no control over her
destiny. Her decision to enter a convent, which Avalle-Arce
calls "a metaphorical death" (Cervantes 1982, 2:39), may
better be seen as a happy ending, as Edwin Williamson suggests (1990, 810). Leonora's decision need not be interpreted
solely in religious terms: the convent was the natural refuge
for a widow without children (Bataillon, 1964, 243). It is a
perfectly reasonable decision, surprising only because nothing she has said or done suggests that she is capable of making it, just as nothing prepares us for Carrizales' act of
forgiveness. Leonora's ability to act wisely does not presup-
pose the ability to explain why she acts as she does. She
could hardly be assigned either a monologue in which she
would debate the different courses of action open to her or a
speech justifying her actions, like the impassioned and yet
coolly reasoned speech in Don Quixote (1.14.185-88) in
which Marcela defends herself against the charge that she is
responsible for Grisóstomo's death (Hart and Rendall 1978).
To allow Leonora to attempt to justify her actions, moreover, would turn the reader away from Carrizales' exemplary act of forgiveness. The story is his, not hers, as the
title makes clear.

Susan Suleiman distinguishes two types of exemplary fictions. One is injunctive, that is, it contains an implicit or
explicit command. It offers not just a meaning (a lesson) but
"a rule of action: its aim . . . is not only to teach something,
but also to influence the receiver's actions or attitudes in a

particular way" (1983, 46). The other, which Suleiman believes is not truly exemplary, does not offer a rule of action but simply depicts some aspect of the world as it is. Most of the *Novelas ejemplares* are of the second kind. *El celoso extremeño* is an exception.

The narrator says that his story is

ejemplo y espejo de lo poco que hay que fiar de llaves, tornos y paredes cuando queda la voluntad libre, y de lo menos que hay que confiar de verdes y pocos años. [2:220]

⟨an example and mirror of how little trust is to be put in keys, locks, and walls when the will remains free, and how much less is to be expected of youth and inexperience.⟩

The rule of action is clear: do not put your trust in locks and keys or in youth and inexperience. But the story does not exemplify this rule: Carrizales placed his trust in locks and keys because he did not trust Leonora, though he had chosen her as a wife precisely because she was young and inexperienced. He is proved wrong on both counts. If it is true that he has been unable to prevent Loaysa from entering his house it is equally true that Leonora, contrary to her husband's expectations, has shown both the will and the ability to defend her honor.

Carrizales himself uses the word *ejemplo* shortly before the narrator's statement just quoted when he tells Leonora, in the presence of her parents and of Marialonso, that he has decided to make a new will:

Porque todo el mundo vea los quilates de la voluntad y fe con que te quise, en este último trance de mi vida quiero mostrarlo de modo que quede en el mundo por ejemplo, si no de bondad, al menos de simplicidad jamás oída ni vista. [2:219]

⟨So that everyone may see the quality of the goodwill and trust with which I loved you, I want this last act of

my life to demonstrate it so that it will be remembered
as an example, if not of goodness, then at least of a foolishness never seen or heard before.⟩

His exemplary act is to call a notary to prepare a new will
that doubles Leonora's dowry and asks her to marry the man
with whom he believes that she has betrayed him.

Carrizales' action is surprising not only because nothing
he has said or done prepares us for it but also because it goes
counter to the expectations produced by the traditional
comic structure of the novella and by his role of *senex iratus*. He is not a complacent cuckold who tolerates his wife's
infidelity or is unaware of it but a husband who accepts responsibility for her action and therefore forgives her. He
does not seek vengeance against Loaysa or Leonora but
against himself:

La venganza que pienso tomar de esta afrenta no es ni
ha de ser de las que ordinariamente suelen tomarse,
pues quiero que así como yo fui extremado en lo que
hice, así sea la venganza que tomaré, tomándola de mí
mismo como del más culpado en este delito. [2:218]

⟨The revenge I intend to take for this affront is not of
the usual kind, for, as I was extreme in what I did, I
want my revenge to be equally so, taking it out on myself as the one most responsible for the offense.⟩

Octavio Paz has observed that "novelty and surprise are
kindred terms, but they are not the same. The conceits,
metaphors, and other verbal devices of the Baroque poem
are designed to amaze; what is new is new if it is unexpected. But seventeenth-century novelty was not critical
nor did it imply the negation of tradition. On the contrary, it
affirmed its continuity. . . . Neither Góngora nor Gracián
was revolutionary in the sense in which we use the word today. . . . For them novelty was synonymous not with change
but with amazement" (1974, 2-3). However true this may be
of Góngora or Quevedo, it hardly applies to Cervantes. Car-

rizales' act of forgiveness is, in Genette's terms, an action without a maxim, one that deliberately goes counter to the prevailing ideology, which demanded that an affront to one's honor must be redressed by causing the death of the person or persons responsible. No doubt it is possible only because Carrizales knows that he is about to die (Bataillon 1964, 242). But even with this limitation it is an extraordinary act, meant to produce admiratio in everyone who hears of it, as Carrizales makes clear when he says that he wants it to be remembered forever as an example. Examples, as Montaigne and Machiavelli knew, impress us by their rarity.

For Montaigne, as John Lyons points out, "novelty and strangeness are sources of value" (1989, 121); "only something that conflicts with what we are accustomed to is worthy of being an example" (ibid.,130). Machiavelli, too, is fond of citing unusual occurrences, *radi esempli;* for him, "a punishment is exemplary to the extent that it *exceeds* the crime being sanctioned" and is seen as " 'excessive and remarkable' " (ibid., 55).

Susan Suleiman has argued that every work of exemplary fiction is characterized by its claim to possess an unequivocal meaning, which need not be stated in the fiction itself. The difficulty is that "there is no such thing as a story that 'expressly entails *a* meaning.' If a story is to be read as having a single specific meaning, it must either be interpreted in a consistent and unambiguous way by the teller, *or* it must exist within a context that invests it with intentionality. Now this context is none other than another text (or a set of other texts), in relation to which the story presents itself as variant or illustration. . . . What we have here, then, is a particular kind of intertextuality" (1983, 43). *El celoso extremeño* is exceptional in that it contains not one but two explicit morals, one provided by the narrator and the other by the protagonist; neither is fully satisfactory in accounting for all the details of the story. I noted in chapter 1 that in most of the other *Novelas ejemplares,* no moral is drawn either by the narrator or by one of the characters. Instead, as Suleiman has written of other exemplary fictions, "the interpretation . . . is inscribed in the internal redundancies of the story *and* in the intertextual context that surrounds it" (1983, 45).

But what is this intertextual context in the case of *El celoso extremeño*? From the perspective of contemporary mores, at least as they are reflected in literature, Carrizales' act of forgiveness is clearly an example of foolishness; from the perspective of Erasmian Christianity, it is just as clearly an example of goodness. Carrizales himself cannot decide between the two interpretations, and the reader is left with an even larger choice between alternative morals to be drawn from the text, as the abundant scholarship on the novella makes clear. Alban Forcione rightly stresses that "the reader is compelled to undergo the enlivening experience of struggling to render intelligible the disturbing elements, of truly collaborating in the creation of the work, and of learning that part of the elusive mystery which it recounts lies in the discovery of the responsibility and the uncomfortable freedom with which the author dignifies him. *El celoso extremeño*, which at first glance appears to be the most formulaic of Cervantes's tales, is in reality one of his most elliptical and elusive" (1982, 91).

CHAPTER 6

Renaissance Dialogue into Novella: *El coloquio de los perros*

In her book on Renaissance genre theory, Rosalie Colie notes that "Aristotle's and Horace's rules for feigning, fiction, and poetry ruled out many of those dignified literary forms beloved of the humanists—the dialogue, the discourse, instructional treatises, utopias, and the like, thus setting up bounds beyond which proper literature should not pass" (1973, 76). She notes also that "as far as *writers* were concerned, rules were there to take or leave—the Renaissance is rich in uncanonical kinds. Many examples of these works are so well written that we find ourselves, as scholars coming so long after, accepting the dialogue, the philosophical poem, to say nothing of prose fictions, as 'literature' " (ibid., 76-77). Thus, both in Rabelais's *Gargantua et Pantagruel* and in Burton's *Anatomy of Melancholy,* "the principal kinds exploited are non-poetic: they carry an early humanist preoccupation into a later age, insisting on elevating to belletristic status kinds which had slipped below the level of artistic attention. In the literature of the late Renaissance there are many examples of such elevation" (ibid., 82). One example Colie might have mentioned is *El coloquio de los perros.*

For a modern reader the title of Cervantes' novella is likely to recall Erasmus' *Colloquia,* as the momentary hesitation about how to interpret the preposition *de*—is the *Coloquio* a dialogue among dogs or about dogs?— recalls Erasmus' title *Moriae Encomium (The Praise of Folly),* or its

Latin variant *Laus stultitiae*. The *Moria*, as Erasmus usually called it, is an oration on the subject of folly delivered by Folly herself; the participants in Cervantes' *Coloquio* are dogs and its subject—one of its many subjects—is a dog's life in a world controlled by men. The first readers of the *Novelas ejemplares* were probably less inclined to associate Cervantes' title with Erasmus. In 1613, when the *Novelas ejemplares* were first published, many of Erasmus' works had been prohibited by the Spanish Inquisition for more than fifty years, although there is good reason to believe that some of them continued to be read. Marcel Bataillon, who has done more than anyone else to trace the fortunes of Erasmus in Spain, declares: "I abandoned long ago the naïve notion that the Index of Prohibited Books, particularly in Spain, caused certain works to disappear forever from the libraries of educated men. The extant examples of these works demonstrate the contrary" (1977, 345). Whether Cervantes' contemporaries connected his title with Erasmus or not, they were certainly familiar with the dialogue as a literary form. According to L. A. Murillo, nearly a thousand dialogues on a wide variety of subjects were written in Spain between 1525 and 1600 (1959, 58); Jacqueline Ferreras places the number considerably higher (1985, 2:1007 n.). Cervantes' contemporaries might still have been surprised by the title *El coloquio de los perros*. Though the second half of the sixteenth century saw the publication in Spain of many books whose titles included the word *Coloquio* or, more often, *Diálogo*, none of them, so far as I know, is a work of narrative fiction.

Campuzano, the protagonist of the preceding novella *El casamiento engañoso* (*The Deceitful Marriage*), insists that the manuscript he urges his friend Peralta to read is almost a literal transciption *(casi por las mismas palabras)* of the conversation between two dogs he overheard while a patient in the Hospital de la Resurrección. He has given it the form of a dialogue in order to avoid having to repeat "Cipión said" and "Berganza answered": "púselo en forma de coloquio por ahorrar de *dijo Cipión, respondió Berganza,* que suele alar-

gar la escritura" (3:238). The title page of the manuscript itself, however, begins with the words *"novela y coloquio* que
pasó entre Cipión y Berganza" (3:241; my italics), novel and
colloquy that took place between Cipión and Berganza. In
giving his work a form that is both novel and colloquy Campuzano, or rather Cervantes, has done more than just sup-
press the tags that identify the speakers.

El coloquio de los perros is formally by far the most complex of the *Novelas ejemplares*. The complexity arises from
Cervantes' elaborate use of the narrative technique of em-
bedding, a favorite with many Baroque writers, in which the
narrator of a story is a character in a story that includes the
story he tells. In Gérard Genette's precise and necessarily
elaborate terminology, such an embedded narrative, a narrative in the second degree, is called metadiegetic (1980,
228). Berganza's story of his life is metadiegetic in relation
to the story written down by Campuzano and read by his
friend Peralta, which in turn is metadiegetic in relation to
that composed by Cervantes. Moreover, Berganza's story includes the witch Cañizares' story of *her* life, which is thus
metadiegetic with respect to Berganza's story.

Still following Genette's analysis of narrative kinds, we
may say that Berganza is a homodiegetic narrator, since he
himself plays a part in the story he tells. More precisely, his
story is an autodiegetic narrative, since he is not merely one
character among others but the story's protagonist (1980,
245). But here, too, complications arise, for in the portion
told by Cañizares, and reported by Berganza in the witch's
own words, he is neither narrator nor protagonist, ceding
both these roles to Cañizares. Berganza takes on the role of
narratee, the one to whom the story is told, so that Cipión
becomes a narratee in the second degree for this portion of
the story. Cañizares' story is thus an autodiogetic narrative
embedded within another autodiegetic narrative that in turn
is embedded within an almost entirely extradiegetic one,
since Campuzano appears in the *Coloquio* only for a moment, and then not by name, when Cipión notices (mistak-
enly) that the soldier is asleep and hence will not overhear

their conversation (3:244-45). Campuzano is both an extradiegetic narrator and a second-degree narratee of the story Berganza thinks he tells only to Cipión. The overall effect is
dizzying, like that of Saul Steinberg's delightful drawing of a
hand drawing the hand that draws it (Gombrich 1960, 238).

By inserting Berganza's account of his life into his night-
long conversation with Cipión Cervantes eliminates one of
the principal features that divide the Renaissance dialogue
from the novel. The dialogue is usually confined to a single
moment of time, though there are exceptions, like Erasmus'
Gerontologia or *Senile Colloquium*, in which several elderly men reminisce about their past lives. Because the *Coloquio* deals primarily with Berganza's adventures, Cervantes
can treat the novelist's essential subject: the transformation
of character by experience. And because Berganza himself
tells the story, Cervantes can invite the reader to consider
not just the dog's adventures but the way he interprets them.

If in its form *El coloquio de los perros* is the most inno-
vative of the *Novelas ejemplares*, in content it is perhaps
the most traditional of the twelve, since it incorporates a
number of popular or traditional anecdotes (*cuentecillos*),
whose importance for an understanding of the literature of
the Siglo de Oro has been demonstrated by Maxime Chevalier (1975, 1978). It is traditional also in another and perhaps
more important sense: several anecdotes are cited by the
dogs in order to make a moral point. The *Coloquio* continues the tradition of the humanist dialogue by including
opinions on a wide variety of subjects, subjects Campuzano
considers varied and important and more appropriate to
men of learning than to dogs, "grandes y diferentes, y más
para ser tratadas por varones sabios que para ser dichas por
bocas de perros" (3:237).

Campuzano is too uncritical in accepting all the dogs'
judgments as worthy of *varones sabios*. Berganza's opinion
of the pastoral romances that so delighted the mistress of
his first master the butcher is a case in point. For Berganza,
these books offer not truth but only entertainment for the
idle: "son cosas soñadas y bien escritas para entretenimiento

de los ociosos, y no verdad alguna" (3:254). Berganza's attack on pastoral, which is sometimes taken as an expression of Cervantes' own views, really serves, as Mary Lee Cozad notes, to reveal that the dog does not understand the nature of literary convention (1988, 178). We shall see later that Berganza is wrong also about much more important matters.

The Renaissance dialogue is a didactic form but it is not a textbook. It does not demand that the reader accept uncritically all the statements made in it. Indeed, he cannot do so, since dialogues typically present interlocutors who hold strongly opposing views. Cervantes characteristically complicates matters by making it impossible for the reader to accept at face value all the statements made by either of the dogs. Carlos Blanco Aguinaga points out that in the *Coloquio* "we no longer find an alternation between contraries presented in opposition to one another from a dogmatic point of view, but an alternation between two points of view, sometimes contrary, sometimes not, which the novelist never judges and about which he never says the last word" (1957, 331). That he does not should not be taken to mean either that Cervantes himself is morally neutral or that he expects his readers to be. I have remarked elsewhere that "Renaissance readers believed that their task was to apply a text to their own particular situations, to use it as a source of guidance in shaping their own moral lives." The reader is not free to interpret the text in any way he likes, since "his search for the significance of the text [will be guided] by his conception of the kind of moral teaching he should seek" (1989, 116-17).

Like many other Renaissance writers, Cervantes believed that literature should instruct as well as delight (Riley 1962, 81-88). One way it can do both at once is to offer the reader a puzzle to be solved, as Cervantes hints in the prologue to the *Novelas ejemplares* with his tantalizing statement that "if it were not that I do not wish to belabor the matter perhaps I would show you the pleasure and benefit (*sabroso y honesto fruto*) that can be drawn from them all together and from each one considered separately" (1:64).

The nature of the pleasure and benefit Cervantes promises in the prologue has been endlessly debated by students of the *Novelas ejemplares*. Bruce Wardropper perhaps defines it best. He sees *tropelías*, a popular form of the word eutrapelia that had come to acquire a different meaning and take on a life of its own, as underlying all twelve of the novellas. A *tropelía* is a magician's trick that makes one thing appear to be another, as the witch Cañizares explains to Berganza (3:292) In the *Novelas ejemplares*, "the trick (*tropelía*) reveals a series of fictional beings who, consciously or not, abandon their place in society only to return to it, apparently inevitably. In the formula usual in the Spanish Golden Age, despite not behaving like themselves, they become once more the persons they really are" (Wardropper 1982, 164).

Tropelías are thus closely related to the Renaissance idea of the flexibility of the self I discussed in chapter 4. In the earlier Renaissance, exemplified by Pico della Mirandola's *Oration on the Dignity of Man*, flexibility means man's freedom to choose his destiny and shape himself into an ideal being. A different conception of flexibility, which becomes dominant in the second half of the sixteenth century though it is found earlier in such writers as Machiavelli, stresses rather man's inability to transform himself. The earlier ideal of vertical flexibility gives way to an ideal of lateral resourcefulness, the ability to adapt oneself to changing circumstances, in the belief, or hope, that, in Machiavelli's words, "se si mutasse con li tempi e con le cose, non si muterebbe fortuna," if one could change with time and circumstances, fortune would never change. A reader of *Don Quixote* will think immediately of Dorotea, who plays so enthusiastically and so well the role of the princess Micomicona and also acts as a skillful advocate of her own cause in persuading Don Fernando that he has both a moral and a legal obligation to marry her (part 1, chapter 36). Cervantes' novel offers plenty of other such skillful improvisers: Altisidora, Ginés de Pasamonte, Sancho in his inspired and successful attempt in part 2, chapter 10, to convince

Don Quixote that a peasant girl is Dulcinea, forcing the knight to suppose that an evil enchanter has prevented him from seeing his lady as she really is.

Berganza, too, possesses a high degree of lateral resourcefulness. He takes on a new role with each new master and proves adept at all of them. His first master, the butcher Nicolás el Romo, teaches him to grab a bull by the ears, and Berganza proudly recalls that he had no difficulty in becoming an expert. With his second master, the shepherd, he proves diligent in protecting the flock; as a watchdog for the merchant he is so successful that his master orders that he be well treated. He is equally good as an aide to the police officer, as the *perro sabio* that the drummer teaches to dance to the sound of his drum and to perform other tricks no other dog could have learned, and as an actor who makes lots of money for his owner.

Berganza is infinitely adaptable, quick to learn whatever each new master requires of him, but like the protagonists of other *Novelas ejemplares*—Preciosa and Don Juan de Cárcamo in *La gitanilla* and their counterparts Costanza and Don Tomás de Avendaño in *La ilustre fregona*—he stubbornly insists on living according to the demands of his own moral code. It is Berganza's insistence on adherence to a rigid moral code that makes it impossible for him to remain for long with any of his masters. Like Don Quixote, Berganza considers it his duty not only to live honorably but to punish those he thinks guilty of wrongdoing, and it is their refusal to accept correction at his hands, or rather jaws, that repeatedly drives him to seek another master who will deserve his loyalty.

Like Don Quixote, Berganza is both lovable and laughable because of his inflexibility. Daniel Javitch has noted the importance that Castiglione's courtiers attach to the moderation and flexibility they associate with *mediocrità*, which "demands that the courtier be ready not only to concede the validity of views contrary to his own but also to moderate his beliefs so that they will accommodate contrary views. . . . The courtiers at Urbino show little tolerance for earnest partisanship or single-mindedness of any kind, but prize instead flexibility" (1983, 19). This kind of flexibility is as lacking in Berganza as it is in Don Quixote.

Purity and strength of will alone are not enough to make a successful reformer. Berganza fails, like Don Quixote, because he cannot or will not see himself as he really is and accept his limitations. His repeated failures to correct the ills he sees in society are due at least in part to his inability to speak. The owner of the sheep does not know that Berganza is trying to warn him against the deceit practiced by the shepherds, nor does the merchant realize that Berganza is trying to protect his master's interests by preventing the nightly meetings of the black servant girl and her lover. Berganza is unable to put into practice something he knows perfectly well in theory: the importance of knowing one's own limitations.

That Berganza knows it in theory is shown by the fable of the lapdog and the ass he cites in the *Coloquio*, commenting that it teaches that actions pleasing in one person may be quite inappropriate in another: "en esta fábula se nos dio a entender que las gracias y donaires de algunos no están bien en otros" (3:260). The same point is made again in the story Berganza tells about one of his last masters, the poet, who assembles the members of a theatrical company to read his new play. The actors give up in disgust before they reach the end of the first act. They are so incensed by the wretched quality of the play that they threaten to attack the poet physically. He leaves, murmuring a phrase that echoes Christ's warning against throwing pearls before swine in the Sermon on the Mount (Matthew 7.6), "No es bien echar las margaritas a los puercos" (3.314). There are other echoes of the sermon in the *novela*. The most obvious is the witch Cañizares' advice to Berganza to practice hypocrisy (3.296), which echoes Matthew 6.5: "And when thou prayest, thou shalt not be as the hypocrites are." It is anticipated by Cipión's rebuke that, if Berganza were a person, he would be a hypocrite, "si tú fueras persona, fueras hipócrita" (3.271). Cipión's warning against *murmuración* (3.267) paraphrases still another passage from the Sermon, "judge not that ye be not judged" (Matthew 7.1), a precept Berganza finds extremely hard to obey.

Like the poet-playwright, Berganza blames his lack of success as a reformer solely on the moral perversity of those who refuse to heed his warnings and not at all on his own shortcomings. Berganza's attempts at reform fail because his inability to use human language disqualifies him for the role he has chosen. His victims see his attempts to punish them only as outbreaks of unprovoked viciousness. They are not wholly wrong in doing so. There is an element of revenge in Berganza's actions, most obvious in his attack on the black girl but apparent also in his relationship to the police officer, that undercuts the moral rightness of his actions, but Berganza himself is quite unaware of this.

Berganza withdraws from the world to enter the service of Mahudes because he believes that the world is irredeemably corrupt. Like Don Quixote's decision to abandon his career as a knight errant, Berganza's withdrawal is based on a failure to grasp the reasons for his lack of success. Don Quixote blames the romances of chivalry rather than his own overliteral reading of them as guides to conduct; Berganza blames the world for resisting his attempts to change it rather than blaming himself for attempting a task to which he is obviously ill suited. Berganza's renunciation of his career as a reformer foreshadows Sancho's renunciation of his ambition to become governor of an *ínsula* in *Don Quixote*, part 2, which appeared in 1615, two years after the publication of the *Novelas ejemplares*. Sancho's decision, like Berganza's, is morally irreproachable but, like Berganza, he comes to it from a misreading of his own experience: he does not realize that the Duke and Duchess have deliberately staged the events of his governorship to see how he will deal with them. Berganza does not see that he fails to change the world not because men are incorrigibly evil but primarily because his inability to speak—more generally, the fact that he is a dog and not a man—makes him ill suited to the role of reformer.

As in his treatment of Sancho in Barataria, Cervantes allows us to contrast Berganza's experiences with the way Berganza himself interprets them. The problematic relationship between an act and the many different ways it can be interpreted is underscored by the role of Cipión, which is largely confined to commenting on the conclusions to be drawn from Berganza's experiences. Although Cipión approves the moral soundness of his friend's decision to withdraw from the world, he, too, fails to see that Berganza's reasons for making it are far from sound. Cipión bears some of the responsibility for Berganza's failure to understand that his inability to speak makes it impossible for him to succeed as a reformer.

Cipión is thus much more than just a narratee, a passive listener. His comments sometimes turn Berganza's narrative from its course; more often, they cause him to return to the story of his adventures after he has digressed. The dialogue differs from the novel, and from more formal treatises on manners or morals, in that it is, or pretends to be, an aleatory form. It purports to present an actual conversation, the beginning and end of which are determined not by the subject under discussion but by external events. Thus, each book of Castiglione's *Book of the Courtier* ends with a decision to postpone the rest of the discussion until the next day because of the lateness of the hour, a convention Cervantes also follows in *El coloquio de los perros*.

The dialogue is an aleatory form also in that no single speaker is in full control of the direction the discussion will take. The result is not anarchy but shared creation; the underlying assumption is that together the participants in a dialogue may discover a truth none of them could have found singly. The philosophical dialogue is thus not just a literary form in which a writer may choose to present his work but a representation of a special way of discovering truth. The connection between dialogue and dialectic, that is, the art of eliciting conclusions by discussion, was made by a number of sixteenth-century writers, as C. J. R. Armstrong points out (1976). In his *Discorso dell'arte del dialogo*

(1585), which Cervantes may have known, Torquato Tasso defines a dialectical discussion as one composed of questions and answers and argues that therefore a person familiar with dialectic is the one best qualified to write dialogues (1982, 28).

As Wayne Booth observes, "one sought, in dialogue, for . . . the assumptions, hardly firm enough to be called principles, found by public testing of opinions . . . that would become no longer *pseudo* once they had been tested communally. . . . In such thinking, nobody thinks alone; . . . Rhetorical thought replaces the 'I' with 'we' " (1983, 131). Humanist dialogues usually imply that a conclusion reached through discussion is correct, but they do not always do so. Hanna Gray notes that "some dialogues were left deliberately without explicit conclusion, either because the author wished to point out what could be said on different sides of doubtful or complex matters, . . . or with the purpose of allowing the reader to render his own final judgment" (1963, 512-13). Cervantes' novella is of this second kind. Cipión's comments sometimes help Berganza to form a more just assessment of his actions, sometimes merely confirm him in his error. The final judgment rests with the reader, as it often does in Cervantes' most characteristic works. Campuzano, or his creator, was right to call the story he offers Peralta a "novela y coloquio."

If the prospects of leading a moral life in the world were as remote as they seem to Berganza and Cipión, then the world-view implicit in the *Coloquio* would indeed be as bleak as it has seemed to some students of the *Novelas ejemplares*. A. A. Parker asserts that "the tone . . . is profoundly serious and sad, not to say bitter" (1956, 21), while L. J. Woodward argues that the lesson of the *Coloquio* is that "the virtuous life is impossible on earth; both witch and dogs find it more profitable to be hypocrites" (1959, 86). Ruth El Saffar similarly believes that "the conclusion at which the dogs arrive is a pessimistic one indeed. They perceive themselves and the society in which they live as hopelessly split, as the spiritual will to growth and transcendence is

severed from the material world of commerce and politics.
The social structure, which maintains itself by power and
hypocrisy, is cut off from the spiritual sources by which it
could be renewed and redeemed" (1976, 82).

We have seen, however, that the moral the dogs draw
from their experiences is questionable. We need not con-
clude that it is impossible for individuals to live useful and
morally exemplary lives or that society is irredeemable. But
to do either demands a sounder understanding of the problems to be solved than that of the dogs—or that of Don
Quixote.

Vicente Lloréns suggests that Cervantes believed not that
the chivalric ideal was absurd but simply that it was irrele-
vant to the problems of the modern world (1967, 222). It is
unlikely that Cervantes felt the same way about the moral
code professed by the dogs. Alban K. Forcione argues persua-
sively that "the Christianity of the *Novelas ejemplares* can
best be understood by recalling Erasmus's Christianity, from
which it may well have derived, and his efforts to sanctify
lay life by urging Christians to bring piety and faith to their
activities, roles, professions, and institutions within society" (1982, 395). Berganza eventually finds a useful, and presumably happy, life in the service of Mahudes. From his
own perspective he withdraws from the world because he
has repeatedly failed to find a master whom he can serve
with full loyalty. From another, and more just perspective,
each new failure is a *felix culpa* that leads him closer to the
appropriately named Hospital de la Resurrección. As E. C.
Riley notes, Berganza sees his work with Mahudes "as a refuge from the moral and social evils of the world—not, the
world being what it is, as a practical cure for them. But it is
a personal solution for Berganza and its general Christian
validity is plain enough" (1976, 197).

Forcione asserts that Cervantes' novella *La fuerza de la
sangre* "confirms the presence of the divine within the secular world, stresses the possibility of man's harmonious
working with God's Providence, and celebrates the value of
human capacities and efforts" (1982, 394-95). Perhaps one

can say the same of the *Coloquio de los perros*. The dogs, however, do not interpret the story of Berganza's life in this way. Neither does Campuzano. He gives no sign that he sees it as having any bearing on his own misadventures, which he has related to Peralta in the metadiegetic narrative embedded in *El casamiento engañoso*. Peralta, although he refuses to believe that his friend really has overheard a conversation between two dogs, is willing to concede the value of the *Coloquio* as a work of imaginative literaerature:

> Yo alcanzo el artificio del *Coloquio* y la invención, y basta. Vámonos al Espolón a recrear los ojos del cuerpo, pues ya he recreado los del entendimiento. [3.322]

> ⟨I appreciate the art and the inventiveness of the *Colloquy*; let the matter rest there. Now let's go to the Espolón to refresh our bodies, since I've already refreshed my understanding.⟩

Peralta's reference to *entendimiento* is perhaps a hint that he sees in the *Coloquio* a significance Campuzano fails to perceive. But it is only a hint. Like the Renaissance humanists whose dialogues may have served him as a point of departure, Cervantes asks his readers to assess critically opposing positions and arguments. In the most enigmatic of the *Novelas ejemplares*, Cervantes demands that his readers exercise their understanding, *los ojos del entendimiento*.

Conclusion

Frank Kermode has defined classics as "old books which people still read." But if classics continue to be read they are not read in the same way: "over and over again in time those old books are accommodated to the sense of readers whose language and culture is different.... The paradox—that there is an identity but that it changes—is made more difficult by the certainty that it can in some measure be redeemed from change, by an effort of interpretation rather than of simple accommodation, the establishment of 'relevance.' It seems that . . . the books we call classics possess intrinsic qualities that endure, but possess also an openness to accommodation which keeps them alive under endlessly varying dispositions" (1983, 43-44).

The *Novelas ejemplares* are classics—old books that people still read—and they have been, and are, read in many different ways. It makes no sense to say that we should read them as Cervantes' contemporaries did. All that we know about the practice of reading in the early seventeenth century suggests that, then as now, individual readers interpreted the same text in different ways, just as it suggests also that a single reader might see a text as teaching different lessons at different times. The secret of the *Novelas ejemplares* is that there is no secret, no single interpretation tacitly endorsed by Cervantes but never openly revealed to his readers.

Kermode observes that "there is a continuing conflict between critics who hold [that] the classic [is] a closed book that learning can partly open, and those who assert that the classic is a more or less open text from which new readings may be generated. . . . The first party requires the reader to use his learning in order to approximate to a reading . . . possible to an informed contemporary of the author's; the second holds that the classic has meanings contemporary with us which, quite possibly, an informed contemporary could not have discovered. The first party practises hermeneutics, the second an extremely elaborate form of accommodation" (1983, 75-76). It will be clear by now that my sympathies in this quarrel lie with the partisans of hermeneutics, though I willingly concede that some of the most interesting recent studies of Cervantes' works view them from Marxist, feminist, or psychoanalytic perspectives unknown to seventeenth-century readers.

I do not mean to imply that present-day readers of the *Novelas ejemplares* ought to share the values held by Cervantes' contemporaries. We need not accept the conception of innate nobility implicit in *La gitanilla*, much less the view, held by many seventeenth-century moralists, both in Spain and elsewhere, that women are morally and intellectually inferior to men. We need only grant that most of Cervantes' contemporaries, though perhaps not Cervantes himself, did not feel as we do about these and many other matters.

Speculations about how old books were read when they were new cannot tell us how we should read them today. Erich Auerbach confronts the problem in the Introduction to his last, posthumously published book: "To grasp the special nature of an epoch or a work, to perceive the nature of the relations between works of art and the time in which they were created, is an endless problem, which each of us . . . must endeavor to solve for himself. . . . Little by little we learn what the various works meant in their own epochs and what they mean in the perspective of the three millennia concerning the literary activity of which we have some knowledge. Lastly, we learn what they mean to us personally, here and now" (1965, 12-13).

Bibliography

Allen, Don Cameron. 1970. *Mysteriously Meant: The Redis-covery of Pagan Symbolism and Allegorical Interpretation in the Renaissance.* Baltimore: Johns Hopkins University Press.

Allen, John J. 1973. *"El celoso extremeño* and *El curioso imperti-nente."* In *Studies in the Spanish Golden Age: Cervantes and Lope de Vega,* ed. Dana B. Drake and José A. Madrigal, 6-11. Miami: Ediciones Universal.

Altman, Ida. 1989. *Emigrants and Society: Extremadura and America in the Sixteenth Century.* Berkeley and Los Angeles: University of California Press.

Amezúa y Mayo, Agustín G. de. 1956-58. *Cervantes creador de la novela corta española.* 2 vols. Valencia: Consejo Superior de Investigaciones Científicas.

Aristotle. 1926. *The "Art" of Rhetoric.* Ed. and trans. John Henry Freese. Loeb Classical Library. Cambridge, Mass.: Harvard University Press.

Armstrong, C. J. R. 1976. "The Dialectical Road to Truth: The Dialogue." *French Renaissance Studies 1540-70: Humanism and the Encyclopedia,* 36-51. Ed. Peter Sharratt. Edinburgh: Edinburgh University Press.

Auerbach, Erich. 1953. *Mimesis: The Representation of Reality in Western Literature.* Trans. Willard R. Trask. Princeton: Princeton University Press.

———. 1965. *Literary Language and Its Public in Late Latin Antiquity and in the Middle Ages.* Trans. Ralph Manheim. New York: Bollingen Foundation.

Bakhtin, M. M. 1981. *The Dialogic Imagination.* Ed. Michael Holquist. Trans. Caryl Emerson and Michael Holquist. Austin: University of Texas Press.

Barber, C. L. 1959. *Shakespeare's Festive Comedy: A Study of Dramatic Form and Its Relationship to Social Custom.* Princeton: Princeton University Press.

Barish, Jonas. 1981. *The Antitheatrical Prejudice.* Berkeley and Los Angeles: University of California Press.

Barrenechea, Ana María. 1961. "*La ilustre fregona* como ejemplo de estructura novelesca cervantina." *Filología* 7:13-32.

Bataillon, Marcel. 1950. *Erasmo y España: estudios sobre la historia espiritual del siglo XVI.* Trans. Antonio Alatorre. Mexico City: Fondo de Cultura Económica.

———. 1964. "Cervantes y el matrimonio cristiano." In *Varia lección de clásicos españoles,* trans. José Pérez Riesco, 238-55. Madrid: Gredos. [First published as "Cervantès et le mariage chrétien," *Bulletin Hispanique* 49 (1947):129-44.]

———. 1977. "Un problema de influencia de Erasmo. El 'Elogio de la locura.' " In *Erasmo y el erasmismo,* trans. Carlos Pujol, 326-46. Barcelona: Crítica.

Bauschatz, Cathleen M. 1980. "Montaigne's Conception of Reading in the Context of Renaissance Poetics and Modern Criticism." In *The Reader in the Text: Essays on Audience and Interpretation,* ed. Susan R. Suleiman and Inge Crosman, 264-91. Princeton: Princeton University Press.

Blanco Aguinaga, Carlos. 1957. "Cervantes y la picaresca: notas sobre dos tipos de realismo." *Nueva revista de filología hispánica* 11:313-42.

———. 1969. "Cervantes and the Picaresque Mode: Notes on Two Kinds of Realism." In *Cervantes: A Collection of Critical Essays,* ed. Lowry Nelson, Jr., 137-51. Englewood Cliffs, N.J.: Prentice-Hall. [A translation by Nelson of pages 313-14, 314-16, and 328-42 of Blanco Aguinaga 1957.]

Booth, Wayne. 1983. "Rhetorical Critics Old and New: The Case of Gérard Genette." In *Reconstructing Literature,* ed. Laurence Lerner, 123-41. Totowa, N.J.: Barnes and Noble.

Borges, Jorge Luis. 1961. *Ficciones.* Buenos Aires: Emecé.

Brown, Jonathan, and J. H. Elliott. 1980. *A Palace for a King: The Buen Retiro and the Court of Philip IV.* New Haven: Yale University Press.

Cascales, Francisco. 1975. *Tablas poéticas.* Ed. Benito Brancaforte. Madrid: Espasa-Calpe.

Castiglione, Baldesar. 1955. "*Il cortegiano*" *con una scelta delle opere minori.* Ed. Bruno Maier. Turin: Unione Tipografico-Editrice Torinese.

———. 1959. *The Book of the Courtier.* Trans. Charles S. Singleton. Garden City: Anchor-Doubleday.

Castro, Américo. 1925. *El pensamiento de Cervantes*. Madrid: Hernando.

Cervantes Saavedra, Miguel de. 1914-17. *Novelas ejemplares*. Ed. Francisco Rodríguez Marín. 2 vols. Madrid: La Lectura.

———. 1928. *"The Spanish Ladie" and Two Other Stories from Cervantes*. Trans. James Mabbe. London: Oxford University Press.

———. 1961. *Six Exemplary Novels*. Trans. Harriet de Onís. Woodbury, New York: Barron.

———. 1962. *Exemplary Stories*. Trans. C. A. Jones. Harmondsworth: Penguin.

———. 1970. *Entremeses*. Ed. Eugenio Asensio. Madrid: Castalia.

———. 1978. *El ingenioso hidalgo Don Quijote de la Mancha*. Ed. Luis Andrés Murillo. 3 vols. Madrid: Castalia.

———. 1982. *Novelas ejemplares*. Ed. Juan Bautista Avalle-Arce. 3 vols. Madrid: Castalia.

Chevalier, Maxime. 1974. "*La Diana* de Montemayor y su público en la España del siglo XVI." In *Creación y público en la literatura española*, ed. J.-F. Botrel and S. Salaün, 40-55. Madrid: Castalia.

———. 1975. *Cuentecillos tradicionales en la España del siglo de oro*. Madrid: Gredos.

———. 1976. *Lectura y lectores en la España de los siglos XVI y XVII*. Madrid: Turner.

———. 1978. *Folklore y literatura: El cuento oral en el siglo de oro*. Madrid: Gredos.

Clamurro, William H. 1982. "*El viejo celoso* y el principio festivo del entremés cervantino." In *Actas del Séptimo Congreso de la Asociación Internacional de Hispanistas celebrado en Venecia del 25 al 30 de agosto de 1980*, 1:317-24. 2 vols. Rome: Bulzoni.

———. 1987. "Identity, Discourse and Social Order in *La ilustre fregona*." *Cervantes* 7:39-56.

———. 1989. "Value and Identity in *La gitanilla*." *Journal of Hispanic Philology* 14:43-60.

Close, Anthony. 1978. *The Romantic Approach to "Don Quixote": A Critical History of the Romantic Tradition in "Quixote" Criticism*. Cambridge: Cambridge University Press.

Cohn, Dorrit. 1978. *Transparent Minds: Narrative Modes for Presenting Consciousness in Fiction*. Princeton: Princeton University Press.

Colie, Rosalie. 1973. *The Resources of Kind: Genre Theory in the Renaissance.* Ed. Barbara K. Lewalski. Berkeley: University of California Press.

Combet, Louis. 1971. *Recherches sur le "refranero" castillan.* Paris: Les Belles Lettres.

Correas, Gonzalo de. 1967. *Vocabulario de refranes y frases proverbiales (1627).* Ed. Louis Combet. Bordeaux: Féret.

Covarrubias, Sebastián de. 1943. *Tesoro de la lengua castellana o española.* Ed. Martín de Riquer. Barcelona: Horta.

Cozad, Mary Lee. 1988. "Cervantes and *Libros de entendimiento.*" *Cervantes* 8:158-82.

Cruickshank, Don. 1978. " 'Literature' and the Book Trade in Golden-Age Spain." *Modern Language Review* 73:799-824.

Dällenbach, Lucien. 1989. *The Mirror in the Text.* Trans. Jeremy Whiteley with Emma Hughes. Chicago: University of Chicago Press. [First published as *Le récit spéculaire: Essai sur la mise en abyme* (Paris: Editions du Seuil, 1977).]

Danto, Arthur C. 1965. *Analytical Philosophy of History.* Cambridge: Cambridge University Press.

Davis, Natalie Zemon. 1987. *Fiction in the Archives: Pardon Tales and Their Tellers in Sixteenth-Century France.* Stanford: Stanford University Press.

Domínguez Ortiz, Antonio. 1971. *The Golden Age of Spain 1516-1639.* Trans. James Casey. London: Weidenfeld and Nicolson.

Dunn, Peter N. 1973. "Las *Novelas ejemplares.*" *Suma cervantina,* ed. J. B. Avalle-Arce and E. C. Riley, 81-118. London: Tamesis.

———. 1982. "Cervantes De/Reconstructs the Picaresque." *Cervantes* 2:109-31.

———. 1985. "Cervantes and the Shape of Experience." *Cervantes* 5:149-61.

El Saffar, Ruth S. 1974. *Novel to Romance: A Study of Cervantes's "Novelas ejemplares".* Baltimore: Johns Hopkins University Press.

———. 1976. *Cervantes: "El casamiento engañoso" and "El coloquio de los perros".* London: Grant and Cutler in association with Tamesis Books.

Elliott, J. H. 1989. *Spain and Its World 1500-1700: Selected Essays.* New Haven: Yale University Press.

Empson, William. 1935. *Some Versions of Pastoral.* London: Chatto and Windus.

Ferreras, Jacqueline. 1985. *Les Dialogues espagnols du XVIe siècle ou L'expression littéraire d'une nouvelle conscience.* 2 vols. Paris: Didier.

———. 1986. "Del diálogo humanístico a la novela." *Homenaje a José Antonio Maravall,* 349-58. Madrid: Consejo Superior de Investigaciones Científicas.

———. 1990. "El diálogo humanístico: Características del género y su reflejo tipográfico, algunas observaciones para futuras ediciones." In *La edición de textos,* ed. Pablo Jauralde, Dolores Noguera, and Alfonso Rey, 451-57. London: Tamesis.

Forcione, Alban K. 1970. *Cervantes, Aristotle, and the "Persiles."* Princeton: Princeton University Press.

———. 1982. *Cervantes and the Humanist Vision: A Study of Four "Exemplary Novels."* Princeton: Princeton University Press.

———. 1984. *Cervantes and the Mystery of Lawlessness: A Study of "El casamiento engañoso y el Coloquio de los perros".* Princeton: Princeton University Press.

———. 1989. "Afterword: Exemplarity, Modernity, and the Discriminating Games of Reading." In *Cervantes's "Exemplary Novels" and the Adventure of Writing,* ed. Michael Nerlich and Nicholas Spadaccini, 331-52. Minneapolis: Prisma Institute.

Fox, Dian. 1983. "The Critical Attitude in *Rinconete y Cortadillo.*" *Cervantes* 3:135-47.

Friedman, Ellen G. 1983. *Spanish Captives in North Africa in the Early Modern Age.* Madison: University of Wisconsin Press.

Frye, Northrop. 1957. *Anatomy of Criticism: Four Essays.* Princeton: Princeton University Press.

———. 1965. *A Natural Perspective: The Development of Shakespearean Comedy and Romance.* New York: Columbia University Press.

———. 1976. *The Secular Scripture: A Study of the Structure of Romance.* Cambridge, Mass.: Harvard University Press.

Genette, Gérard. 1969. "Vraisemblance et motivation." In *Figures II,* 71-99. Paris: Editions du Seuil.

———. 1980. *Narrative Discourse: An Essay in Method.* Trans. Jane E. Lewin. Ithaca: Cornell University Press.

Gilman, Stephen. 1989. *The Novel According to Cervantes.* Berkeley: University of California Press.

Gombrich, E. H. 1960. *Art and Illusion: A Study in the Psychology of Pictorial Representation.* New York: Pantheon Books for Bollingen Foundation.

Gray, Hanna H. 1963. "Renaissance Humanism: The Pursuit of Eloquence." *Journal of the History of Ideas* 24:497-514.

Greene, Thomas. 1968. "The Flexibility of the Self in Renaissance Literature." In *The Disciplines of Criticism: Essays in Literary Theory, Interpretation, and History*, ed. Peter Demetz, Thomas Greene, and Lowry Nelson, Jr., 241-64. New Haven: Yale University Press.

Guillén, Claudio. 1971. *Literature as System: Essays toward the Theory of Literary History.* Princeton: Princeton University Press.

Hainsworth, G. 1933. *Les "Novelas ejemplares" de Cervantes en France au XVIIe siècle.* Paris: Champion.

Hampton, Timothy. 1990. *Writing from History: The Rhetoric of Exemplarity in Renaissance Literature.* Ithaca: Cornell University Press.

Hart, Thomas R. 1979. "Cervantes' Sententious Dogs." *MLN* 94:377-86.

———. 1981. "Versions of Pastoral in Three *Novelas ejemplares*." *Bulletin of Hispanic Studies* 58:283-91.

———. 1988. "La ejemplaridad de *El amante liberal*." *Nueva revista de filología hispánica* 36:303-18.

———. 1989. *Cervantes and Ariosto: Renewing Fiction.* Princeton: Princeton University Press.

———. 1990. "Renaissance Dialogue into Novel: Cervantes' *Coloquio*." *MLN* 105:191-202.

———. 1991. "La novela y el *romance* en el *Quijote*." *Insula*, no. 538 (October, 1991):21, 23.

———. 1992. "¿Cervantes perspectivista?" *Nueva revista de filología hispánica* 40:293-303.

Hart, Thomas R. and Steven Rendall. 1978. "Rhetoric and Persuasion in Marcela's Address to the Shepherds." *Hispanic Review* 46:287-98.

Heliodorus. 1954. *Historia etiópica de los amores de Teágenes y Cariclea.* Trans. Fernando de Mena [1587]. Ed. Francisco López Estrada. Madrid: Real Academia Española. [Includes a Spanish version of Jacques Amyot's preface to his translation, *L'Histoire aethiopique de Heliodorus*, Paris, 1547.]

Herrero, Javier. 1987. "Emerging Realism: Love and Cash in *La ilustre fregona.* In *From Dante to García Márquez: Studies in Romance Literatures and Linguistics Presented to Anson Conant Piper*, ed. Gene H. Bell-Villada, Antonio Giménez, and George Pistorius, 47-59. Williamstown, Mass.: Williams College.

Ife, B. W. 1985. *Reading and Fiction in Golden-Age Spain: A Platonist Critique and Some Picaresque Replies*. Cambridge: Cambridge University Press.

Jakobson, Roman. 1987. *Language in Literature*. Ed. Krystyna Pomorska and Stephen Rudy. Cambridge, Mass.: Belknap Press of Harvard University Press.

Javitch, Daniel. 1983. *"Il cortegiano* and the Constraints of Despotism." In *Castiglione: The Ideal and the Real in Renaissance Culture*, ed. Robert W. Hanning and David Rosand, 17-28. New Haven: Yale University Press.

————. 1991. *Proclaiming a Classic: The Canonization of "Orlando furioso"*. Princeton: Princeton University Press.

Johnston, Robert M. 1980. "Picaresque and Pastoral in *La ilustre fregona*." In *Cervantes and the Renaissance*, ed. Michael D. McGaha, 167-77. Easton, Pa. Juan de la Cuesta.

Joly, Monique. 1982. "Monipodio Revisited." In *Actas del Séptimo Congreso de la Asociación Internacional de Hispanistas celebrado en Venecia del 25 al 30 de agosto de 1980*, 2:603-11. 2 vols. Rome: Bulzoni.

————. 1983. "Para una reinterpretación de *La ilustre fregona*: ensayo de tipología cervantina." *Aureum Saeculum Hispanum: Beiträge zu Texten des Siglo de Oro: Festschrift für Hans Flasche zum 70. Geburtstag*, ed. Karl-Hermann Körner and Dietrich Briesemeister, 103-116. Wiesbaden: F. Steiner.

Jones, Joseph R. 1985. "Cervantes y la virtud de la *eutrapelia:* la moralidad de la literatura de esparcimiento." *Anales cervantinos* 23:19-30.

Kahn, Victoria. 1985. *Rhetoric, Prudence, and Skepticism in the Renaissance*. Ithaca: Cornell University Press.

Keightley, Ronald G. 1982. "The Narrative Structure of *Rinconete y Cortadillo*." In *Essays on Narrative Fiction in the Iberian Peninsula in Honour of Frank Pierce*, ed. R. B. Tate, 39-54. Oxford: Dolphin.

Kermode, Frank. 1983. *The Classic: Literary Images of Permanence and Change*. Cambridge, Mass.: Harvard University Press.

————. 1985. *Forms of Attention*. Chicago: University of Chicago Press.

Lambert, A. F. 1980. "The Two Versions of Cervantes' *El celoso extremeño:* Ideology and Criticism." *Bulletin of Hispanic Studies* 57:219-31.

Lanham, Richard A. 1965. "The Old *Arcadia.*" In Walter R. Davis and Richard A. Lanham, *Sidney's "Arcadia"*, 183-417. New Haven: Yale University Press.

Leblon, Bernard. 1985. *Les Gitans d'Espagne: Le prix de la différence.* Paris: Presses Universitaires de France.

León, Fray Luis de. 1951. *La perfecta casada.* In *Obras completas castellanas,* 2d ed., ed. P. Félix García, O.S.A., 233-342. Madrid: Editorial Católica.

Lerner, Isaías. 1980. "Marginalidad en las *Novelas ejemplares:* I. *La gitanilla.*" *Lexis* 4:47-59.

Lipmann, Stephen H. 1986. "Revision and Exemplarity in Cervantes' *El celoso extremeño.*" *Cervantes* 6:113-21.

Lloréns, Vicente. 1967. "La intención del *Quijote.*" *Literatura, historia, política.* Madrid: Revista de Occidente.

Lowe, Jennifer. 1970. *Cervantes: Two "Novelas ejemplares": La gitanilla* [and] *La ilustre fregona.* London: Grant and Cutler.

———. 1970-71. "A Note on Cervantes' *El amante liberal.*" *Romance Notes* 12:400-03.

Lyons, John D. 1989. *Exemplum: The Rhetoric of Example in Early Modern France and Italy.* Princeton: Princeton University Press.

McKendrick, Melveena. 1980. *Cervantes.* Boston: Little, Brown.

———. 1984. "Honour/Vengeance in the Spanish 'Comedia': A Case of Mimetic Transference?" *Modern Language Review* 79:313-35.

McKeon, Michael. 1987. *The Origins of the English Novel 1600-1740.* Baltimore: Johns Hopkins University Press.

Maclean, Ian. 1980. *The Renaissance Notion of Woman.* Cambridge: Cambridge University Press.

Maravall, José Antonio. 1986. *Culture of the Baroque: Analysis of a Historical Structure.* Trans. Terry Cochran. Minneapolis: University of Minnesota Press.

Molho, Maurice. 1990. "Aproximación al *Celoso extremeño.*" *Nueva revista de filología hispánica* 38:743-92.

Molière. 1968. *L'Ecole des femmes* and *La critique de "L'Ecole des femmes.*" Ed. W. D. Howarth. Oxford: Basil Blackwell.

Montaigne, Michel de. *Essais.* 1924. Reprint 1965. Ed. Pierre Villey. Paris: Presses Universitaires de France.

———. 1958. *The Complete Works of Montaigne.* Trans. Donald M. Frame. Stanford, Calif.: Stanford University Press.

Murillo, L. A. 1959. "Diálogo y dialéctica en el siglo XVI español." *Revista de la Universidad de Buenos Aires,* 5th ser. 4:56-66.

———. 1961. "Cervantes' *Coloquio de los perros,* A Novel-Dialogue." *Modern Philology* 58:174-85.

Nelson, William. 1973. *Fact or Fiction: The Dilemma of the Renaissance Storyteller.* Cambridge, Mass.: Harvard University Press.

Neuschäfer, Hans-Jörg. 1990. "*El curioso impertinente* y la tradición de la novelística europea." *Nueva revista de filología hispánica* 38:605-20.

Olson, Elder. 1968. *The Theory of Comedy.* Bloomington: Indiana University Press.

Parker, A. A. 1956. *Valor actual del humanismo español.* Madrid: Ateneo.

———. 1967. *Literature and the Delinquent: The Picaresque Novel in Spain and Europe 1599-1753.* Edinburgh: Edinburgh University Press.

Paz, Octavio. 1974. *Children of the Mire: Modern Poetry from Romanticism to the Avant-Garde.* Trans. Rachel Phillips. Cambridge, Mass.: Harvard University Press.

———. 1988. *Sor Juana, or The Traps of Faith.* Trans. Margaret Sayers Peden. Cambridge, Mass.: Belknap Press of Harvard University Press.

Perry, Mary Elizabeth. 1980. *Crime and Society in Early Modern Seville.* Hanover, N. H.: University Press of New England.

Pierce, Frank. 1953. "Reality and Realism in the *Exemplary Novels.*" *Bulletin of Hispanic Studies* 30:134-42.

———. 1977. "*La gitanilla:* A Tale of High Romance." *Bulletin of Hispanic Studies* 54:283-95.

Pike, Ruth. 1972. *Aristocrats and Traders: Sevillian Society in the Sixteenth Century.* Ithaca: Cornell University Press.

Pitt-Rivers, J. A. 1961. *The People of the Sierra.* University of Chicago Press.

———. 1966. "Honour and Social Status." In *Honour and Shame: The Values of Mediterranean Civilization,* ed. J. G. Peristiany. Chicago: University of Chicago Press.

Poggioli, Renato. 1975. *The Oaten Flute: Essays on Pastoral Poetry and the Pastoral Ideal.* Cambridge, Masssachusetts: Harvard University Press.

Rahner, Hugo. 1972. "Eutrapelia: A Forgotten Virtue." In *Man at Play,* 91-105. New York: Herder and Herder.

Rendall, Steven. 1979. "*Mus in Pice:* Montaigne and Interpretation." *MLN* 94:1056-71.

———. 1992. *Distinguo: Reading Montaigne Differently.* Oxford: Clarendon Press.

Riley, E. C. 1962. *Cervantes's Theory of the Novel.* Oxford: Clarendon Press.

———. 1963. "Aspectos del concepto de *admiratio* en la teoría literaria del siglo de oro." In *Studia philologica: Homenaje ofrecido a Dámaso Alonso por sus amigos y discípulos con ocasión de su 60.º aniversario* 3:173-83.

———. 1976. "Cervantes and the Cynics (*El licenciado Vidriera* and *El coloquio de los perros*)." *Bulletin of Hispanic Studies* 53:189-99.

———. 1981. "Cervantes: A Question of Genre." In *Mediaeval and Renaissance Studies on Spain and Portugal in Honour of P. E. Russell,* ed. F. W. Hodcroft et al., 69-85. Oxford: Society for the Study of Mediaeval Languages and Literature.

———. 1986. *Don Quixote.* London: Allen and Unwin.

———. 1989. "Romance, the Picaresque and *Don Quixote I.*" In *Studies in Honor of Bruce W. Wardropper,* ed. Dian Fox et al., 237-48. Newark, Del.: Juan de la Cuesta.

Romeu Figueras, José, ed. 1965. *Cancionero musical de palacio (siglos XV-XVI).* 2 vols. Barcelona: Consejo Superior de Investigaciones Cientificas—Instituto Español de Musicología.

Rosenblat, Angel. 1971. *La lengua del "Quijote."* Madrid: Gredos.

Russell, P. E. 1953. "A Stuart Hispanist: James Mabbe." *Bulletin of Hispanic Studies* 30:75-84.

———. 1969. "*Don Quixote* as a Funny Book." *Modern Language Review* 64:312-26.

———. 1978. "El Concilio de Trento y la literatura profana: reconsideración de una teoría." In *Temas de "La Celestina" y otros estudios,* 443-78. Barcelona: Ariel.

———. 1985. *Cervantes.* Oxford: Oxford University Press.

Scholes, Robert and Robert Kellogg. 1966. *The Nature of Narrative.* New York: Oxford University Press.

Smith, Hallett. 1952. *Elizabethan Poetry: A Study in Conventions, Meaning, and Expression.* Cambridge, Mass.: Harvard University Press.

Sobejano, Gonzalo. 1978. "Sobre tipología y ordenación de las *Novelas ejemplares.*" *Hispanic Review* 46:65-75.

Stagg, Geoffrey. 1984. "The Refracted Image: Porras and Cervantes." *Cervantes* 4:139-53.

Stevens, Wallace. 1965. *The Necessary Angel: Essays on Reality and the Imagination.* New York: Alfred A. Knopf.

Suleiman, Susan Rubin. 1983. *Authoritarian Fictions: The Ideological Novel as a Literary Genre.* New York: Columbia University Press.

Tasso, Torquato. 1982. *Discorso dell' arte del dialogo.* In *Tasso's Dialogues: A Selection with the "Discourse on the Art of the Dialogue,"* trans. Carnes Lord and Dain A. Trafton, 16-41. Berkeley: University of California Press.

Thompson, Stith. 1955-58. *Motif-Index of Folk-Literature.* 6 vols. Bloomington: Indiana University Press.

Torner, Eduardo M. 1966. *Lírica hispánica: Relaciones entre lo popular y lo culto.* Madrid: Castalia.

Trueblood, Alan. 1989. "The Art of Dialogue in the Early Seventeenth Century: Two Examples." In *Studies in Honor of Bruce W. Wardropper,* ed. Dian Fox et al., 347-58. Newark, Del.: Juan de la Cuesta.

Varela, José Luis. 1968. "Sobre el realismo cervantino en *Rinconete.*" *Atlántida* 6:434-49.

Vickers, Brian. 1988. *In Defence of Rhetoric.* Oxford: Clarendon Press.

Vilanova, Antonio. 1949. "El peregrino andante en el *Persiles* de Cervantes." *Boletín de la Real Academia de Buenas Letras de Barcelona* 22:97-159.

Wallace, John M. 1974. " 'Examples Are Best Precepts': Readers and Meanings in Seventeenth-Century Poetry." *Critical Inquiry* 2:273-90

Wardropper, Bruce W. 1981. "Ambiguity in *El viejo celoso.*" *Cervantes* 1:19-27.

———. 1982. "La eutrapelia en las *Novelas ejemplares* de Cervantes." In *Actas del Séptimo Congreso de la Asociación Internacional de Hispanistas celebrado en Venecia del 25 al 30 de agosto de 1980,* 1:153-69. 2 vols. Rome: Bulzoni.

Watt, Ian. 1957. *The Rise of the Novel.* Berkeley: University of California Press.

———. 1982. "Elizabethan Fiction." In *The New Pelican Guide to English Literature,* ed. Boris Ford, vol. 2, *The Age of Shakespeare,* 195-206. Harmondsworth: Penguin.

Weber, Alison. 1979. "*La ilustre fregona* and the Barriers of Caste." *Papers on Language and Literature* 15:73-81.

Weinberg, Bernard. 1961. *A History of Literary Criticism in the Italian Renaissance.* 2 vols. Chicago: University of Chicago Press.

Whinnom, Keith. 1980. "The Problem of the 'Best-Seller' in Spanish Golden-Age Literature." *Bulletin of Hispanic Studies* 57:189-98.

———. 1982. "The *Historia de Duobus Amantibus* of Aeneas Sylvius Piccolomini and the Development of Spanish Golden-Age Fiction." In *Essays on Narrative Fiction in the Iberian Peninsula in Honour of Frank Pierce*, ed. R. B. Tate, 243-55. Oxford: Dolphin.

Williamson, Edwin. 1984. *The Half-Way House of Fiction: "Don Quixote" and Arthurian Romance*. Oxford: Clarendon Press.

———. 1990. "El 'misterio escondido' en *El celoso extremeño*: una aproximación al arte de Cervantes." *Nueva revista de filología hispánica* 38:793-815.

Wilson, Diana de Armas. 1991. *Allegories of Love: Cervantes's "Persiles and Sigismunda."* Princeton: Princeton University Press.

Wiltrout, Ann E. 1981. "Role Playing and Rites of Passage: *La ilustre fregona* and *La gitanilla*." *Hispania* 64:388-99.

Wolff, Samuel Lee. 1912. *The Greek Romances in Elizabethan Prose Fiction*. New York: Columbia University Press.

Woodward, L. J. 1959. "*El casamiento engañoso y el coloquio de los perros*." *Bulletin of Hispanic Studies* 36:80-87.

Index